SpringerBriefs in Law

More information about this series at http://www.springer.com/series/10164

Markus Kaltenborn

Social Rights and International Development

Global Legal Standards for the Post-2015 Development Agenda

Springer

Markus Kaltenborn
Faculty of Law
Ruhr-Universität Bochum
Bochum
Germany

ISSN 2192-855X ISSN 2192-8568 (electronic)
ISBN 978-3-662-45351-3 ISBN 978-3-662-45352-0 (eBook)
DOI 10.1007/978-3-662-45352-0

Library of Congress Control Number: 2014954068

Springer Heidelberg New York Dordrecht London

Printed on acid-free paper

Springer is part of Springer Science+Business Media (www.springer.com)

Contents

Abbreviations

ACHPR	African Commission on Human and Peoples' Rights
ACWC	ASEAN Commission on the Promotion and Protection of the Rights of Women and Children
AFDI	Annuaire Français de Droit International
AICHR	ASEAN Intergovernmental Commission on Human Rights
AJIL	American Journal of International Law
ASEAN	Association of Southeast Asian Nations
ASF	Avocats Sans Frontières
ATCA	Alien Tort Claims Act
AU	African Union
AVR	Archiv des Völkerrechts
BMZ	Bundesministerium für wirtschaftliche Zusammenarbeit und Entwicklung
CEDAW	Convention on the Elimination of All Forms of Discrimination against Women
CESCR	Committee on Economic, Social and Cultural Rights
CMW	International Convention on the Protection of the Rights of All Migrant Workers and Members of Their Families
CRC	Convention on the Rights of the Child
CRPD	Convention on the Rights of Persons with Disabilities
CSR	Corporate Social Responsibility
DAC	OECD Development Assistance Committee
DFID	Department for International Development
ECOSOC	United Nations Economic and Social Council
EIDHR	European Instrument for Democracy and Human Rights
EJIL	European Journal of International Law
FAO	Food and Agriculture Organization
FCO	Foreign and Commonwealth Office
FES	Friedrich-Ebert-Stiftung
GATS	General Agreement on Trade in Services

GFSP	Global Food Safety Partnership
GIGA	German Institute for Global and Area Studies
GIZ	Deutsche Gesellschaft für Internationale Zusammenarbeit
GoJIL	Göttingen Journal of International Law
GYIL	German Yearbook of International Law
HILJ	Harvard International Law Journal
HLP	High-Level Panel of Eminent Persons on the Post-2015 Development Agenda
HLPE	High-Level Panel of Experts on Food Security and Nutrition
HLR	Harvard Law Review
HRC	Human Rights Council
HRLR	Human Rights Law Review
HRQ	Human Rights Quarterly
IACHR	Inter-American Commission on Human Rights
IBRD	International Bank for Reconstruction and Development
ICC	International Criminal Court
ICCPR	International Covenant on Civil and Political Rights
ICESCR	International Covenant on Economic, Social and Cultural Rights
ICJ	International Court of Justice/Statute of the ICJ
ICLQ	International and Comparative Law Quarterly
IDA	International Development Association
ILA	International Law Association
ILC	International Law Commission
ILO	International Labour Organization
IMF	International Monetary Fund
INEF	Institut für Entwicklung und Frieden
IOE	International Organisation of Employers
ISSA	International Social Security Association
JWT	Journal of World Trade
LDCs	Least Developed Countries
LJIL	Leiden Journal of International Law
MDG	Millennium Development Goal
MPEPIL	Max Planck Encyclopedia of Public International Law
NGO	Non-Governmental Organization
NHIA	National Health Insurance Authority
NILR	Netherlands International Law Review
NorJIL	Nordic Journal of International Law
NQHR	Netherlands Quarterly of Human Rights
NYIL	Netherlands Yearbook of International Law
OAS	Organization of American States
OAU	Organization of African Unity
ODA	Official Development Assistance
ODI	Overseas Development Institute
OECD	Organization for European Co-operation and Development
OHCHR	Office of the High Commissioner for Human Rights

OP	Optional Protocol to the ICESCR
P4H	Providing for Health
PPA	Programme Partnership Arrangement
PRSP	Poverty Reduction Strategy Paper
RGDIP	Revue Générale de Droit International Public
RIW	Recht der internationalen Wirtschaft
SPF	Social Protection Floor
SWP	Stiftung Wissenschaft und Politik
TRIPS	Agreement on Trade-Related Aspects of Intellectual Property Rights
UDHR	Universal Declaration of Human Rights
UN	United Nations/United Nations Charter
UN Doc	Document of the United Nations
UN GA	General Assembly of the United Nations
UNCHR	United Nations Commission on Human Rights
UNDG	United Nations Development Group
UNDP	United Nations Development Programme
UNHCHR	United Nations High Commissioner for Human Rights
UNICEF	United Nations Children's Fund
UNRISD	United Nations Research Institute for Social Development
UNTS	United Nations Treaty Series
UPR	Universal Periodic Review
USAID	United States Agency for International Development
USC	United States Code
VRÜ	Verfassung und Recht in Übersee
VUWLR	Victoria University of Wellington Law Review
WHA	World Health Assembly
WHO	World Health Organization
WTO	World Trade Organization
ZaöRV	Zeitschrift für ausländisches öffentliches Recht und Völkerrecht
ZSchwR	Zeitschrift für Schweizerisches Recht

Chapter 1
Introduction: Social Rights as a Legal Framework for International Development Strategies

Abstract Poverty is not only an economic and sociopolitical problem of individual States and societies, but also a global challenge with which the whole community of States is confronted. This book focuses particularly on the role which international human rights law has to take in coping with this challenge. The governments of developing and newly industrializing countries have to do everything in their power to enable their population to conduct a life in accordance with respect for basic social human rights. But also the governments of the developed countries are legally obliged to respect these rights in the design of their political programs (economic policy, foreign affairs, development aid).

Keywords Global poverty reduction · Social rights · Legal obligations of developing and developed countries · Links between development policy and human rights

When "severe violations of human rights" are bemoaned by the media in a given country, they mostly refer to the abuse of political and civil rights: demonstrations are restricted; journalists are barred from doing their job; and political dissidents are imprisoned without a fair trial, or even threatened with torture or the death penalty. A multitude of other, similar serious infringements of liberty are dominant in the news coverage on human rights. Less prominent, however, is the fact that the protection of another group of human rights, namely social rights, is restricted to an even larger extent in most countries of the world on a daily basis. Although considerable progress has been made in global poverty reduction, data published annually by the *United Nations* on the implementation status of the *Millennium Development Goals* (MDGs) are still cause for alarm: About one in five persons in developing countries (mostly in sub-Saharan Africa and Southern Asia) lives below the poverty line, i.e. these people must survive on less than 1,25 USD a day.[1] Generally, this means that these people suffer from hunger and malnutrition, have little or no access to primary health care services, in most cases inappropriate accommodation and, in addition, insufficient or non-existent social protection.

[1] United Nations 2014, p. 7.

M. Kaltenborn, *Social Rights and International Development*,
SpringerBriefs in Law, DOI 10.1007/978-3-662-45352-0_1

It is certain that these are not only the economic and socio-political problems of individual States and societies, but are also global challenges with which the whole community of States is confronted.[2] Ever since the *International Covenant on Economic, Social and Cultural Rights* (ICESCR) came into force in 1976, giving worldwide recognition to social and economic rights, this issue has also been developing into a serious *legal* problem for the South as well as the North: The governments of developing and newly industrializing countries are bound by international law to guarantee basic minimum standards of welfare within their sphere of responsibility. *They* are, in the first instance, addressees for claims arising from the violation of social human rights—therefore they have to do everything in their power to enable their population to conduct a life in accordance with respect for basic social human rights. However, governments of the northern hemisphere also bear not only political, but also legal responsibility for overcoming global poverty, because it is their duty to align consistently their relationships with the countries of the South with the requirements of the human rights treaties.[3] Most notably, this means that their development cooperation programs must be designed in accordance with social rights, hence turning poverty reduction into the main focus of international aid.

Nonetheless, during the second half of the last century, development policy and human rights protection have remained fields of action whose convergence has been limited—thus depicted by Philip Alston as "ships passing in the night".[4] This relationship has only recently changed fundamentally: Human rights are increasingly becoming a focus of development policy objectives.[5] In particular, the MDGs and their emphasis on global poverty reduction have led to the ever-growing importance of social human rights in the current development policy debates. Other global initiatives, such as the recent adoption of the *Social Protection Floors Recommendation* by the *International Labour Conference* in 2012, have contributed additional momentum to the further specification and implementation of global social legal standards.

It is the aim of this study to provide an overview of the global protection of social rights and to highlight its importance for the discussion on the future orientation of development cooperation.[6] Therefore, an initial analysis of the relevant

---

[2] Other agreements ensuring social human rights had already been adopted before 1966 (see infra Sect. 2.2). Nevertheless, these agreements have not received global support, whereas today the ICESCR is binding for almost all States.

[3] This will be discussed later in more detail, cf. Sect 3.3.

[4] Alston 2005; see also Archer 2009; Marks 2001.

[5] For the relationship between human rights and development cooperation see the concise overview in Dann 2012, pp. 93–99, 233–259; see also contributions in Alston and Robinson 2005; and in Andreassen and Marks 2010.

[6] In some parts this study is based on previous work that has been published (in German) in Kaltenborn 2014. I would like to thank Lisa Gow, LLB University of Strathclyde (Glasgow), and Annika Engelbert, PhD candidate at the Institute of Development Research and Development Policy (IEE) of Ruhr-Universität Bochum, very much for their helpful comments on the English version of this text.

sources of law and implementation mechanisms is necessary (Chap. 2), as well as the presentation of the main legal obligations arising from international recognition of social rights (Chap. 3). In the following, the content of some specific social rights in the context of development cooperation will be examined (Chap. 4). Finally, newer global initiatives, linking development policy issues to human rights perspectives, will be presented (Chap. 5); they offer guidance for the future design of North-South relations that are currently under discussion in the frame of the *Post-2015 Development Agenda.*

References

Alston Ph (2005) Ships Passing in the Night. The Current State of the Human Rights and Development Debate seen through the lens of the Millennium Development Goals. HRQ 25:755–829

Alston Ph, Robinson M (eds) (2005) Human Rights and Development: Towards mutual reinforcement. Oxford University Press, Oxford

Andreassen BA, Marks St P (eds) (2010) Development as a Human Right: Legal, Political and Economic Dimensions, 2nd edn. Intersentia, Antwerp

Archer R (2009) Linking Rights and Development: Some Critical Challenges. In: Hickey S, Mitlin D (eds) Rights-Based Approaches to Development: Exploring the Potential and Pitfalls. Kumarian Press, Sterling, pp 21–30

Dann Ph (2012) Entwicklungsverwaltungsrecht. Theorie und Dogmatik des Rechts der Entwicklungszusammenarbeit, untersucht am Beispiel der Weltbank, der EU und der Bundesrepublik Deutschland. Mohr Siebeck, Tübingen (English version 2013: The Law of Development Cooperation. A comparative analysis of the World Bank, the EU and Germany. Cambridge University Press, Cambridge)

Kaltenborn M (2014) Soziale Rechte und Entwicklung. In: Dann Ph et al (eds) Entwicklung und Recht. Nomos, Baden-Baden, pp 149–181

Marks St P (2001) The Human Rights Framework for Development: Seven Approaches. Working Paper Series of the François-Xavier Bagnoud Center for Health and Human Right, Boston. http://www.crin.org/docs/resources/publications/hrbap/Seven_approaches_RBA.pdf. Accessed 3 Sept 2014

United Nations (2014) The Millennium Development Goals Report 2014. United Nations, New York. http://www.un.org/millenniumgoals/2014%20MDG%20report/MDG%202014%20English%20web.pdf. Accessed 3 Sept 2014

Chapter 2
Legal Sources of Social Rights and Implementation Mechanisms at the International Level

Abstract When searching for the "sources" of social human rights at the international level, the canon of sources of international law, as stipulated in Article 38ICJ, is an obvious starting-point. According to this provision, international treaties are particularly significant—these can be treaties ratified at both the global (see Sects. 2.1–2.3) and regional level (Sect. 2.4), treaties containing statements on social rights in general (such as the *UN International Covenant on Economic, Social and Cultural Rights*, which will be discussed further under Sect. 2.1), and finally those concerning particular topics with references to individual social rights (Sect. 2.2). All these treaties have in common the fact that they include certain mechanisms (procedures, institutions) for the national implementation of the international obligations. An additional source of international law worthy of consideration in relation to social rights is customary international law, whose practical implications in the field of human rights, however, have receded into the background. Instead, the multifaceted *soft law* documents of international organizations working on development issues have recently gained increasing importance: Although these documents do not constitute sources of international law in the narrower sense, they have a significant influence on the normative advancement of social human rights and their implementation on the national level (Sect. 2.5).

Keywords International Covenant on Economic, Social and Cultural Rights (ICESCR) · Optional Protocol to the ICESCR · Special human rights treaties · Human Rights Council · Independent experts · Regional protection of human rights · Soft law

M. Kaltenborn, *Social Rights and International Development*,
SpringerBriefs in Law, DOI 10.1007/978-3-662-45352-0_2

2.1 The International Covenant on Economic, Social and Cultural Rights

The *International Covenant on Economic, Social and Cultural Rights* of 1966 (ICESCR)[1] is nowadays indeed the most important, but not the first legal document attending to the protection of social rights on the global level. Almost two decades earlier, some basic social rights had already been prescribed in the *Universal Declaration of Human Rights* (UDHR), for example the right to social security in Article 22, and the rights to food, clothing, housing, medical care and necessary social services in Article 25. While these social rights are today globally considered to be part of customary international law,[2] their enshrinement and clarification in treaty law has received (almost) global recognition via the ICESCR. The ICESCR now has 162 States Parties, hence most States in the world are legally bound to the obligations listed in the treaty.[3] Indeed, some of the States Parties' approvals are subject to certain reservations, but very few of these caveats are sufficiently far-reaching to lead to considerable restrictions on the protection of social rights.[4]

The Covenant of 1966 does not distinguish clearly between the individual groups of human rights. However, there is large consensus that, on the one hand, "economic rights" entail the right to work (Article 6 ICESCR) and the right to just and favourable working conditions (Article 7 ICESCR), as well as the right to form or join trade unions (including the right to strike, Article 8 ICESCR). On the other hand, "cultural rights", as defined by ICESCR, comprise the right to education (Articles 13, 14 ICESCR) and the right to participation in cultural life (Article 15 ICESCR). The ICESCR guarantees the following "social rights":

- the right to social security (Article 9 ICESCR);
- the social protection of the family, mothers, children and young persons (Article 10 ICESCR);

---

[1] 993 UNTS 3, https://treaties.un.org/Pages/ViewDetails.aspx?src=TREATY&mtdsg_no=IV-3&chapter=4&lang=en. For an introduction to the main provisions see Riedel 2011.—All websites cited in this chapter have been last accessed 3 September 2014.

[2] As a resolution of an international organization, the UDHR is not a legally binding document; nevertheless many authors—quite rightly—assume that (most of) its provisions have meanwhile achieved the status of international customary law (see the references in Kälin and Künzli 2009, p. 71, note 98). For the debate on the customary law status of the UDHR see also Hannum 1995; Hillgenberg 1999, p. 505; Buergenthal 2007, para 9; von Bernstorff 2008, p. 913; McBeth et al. 2011, pp. 22–24; Crawford 2012, pp. 279–280; Bantekas and Oette 2013, pp. 62–63; with regard to the basic social rights Salomon 2013, p. 270.

[3] The most prominent and well-known exemption is the United States which have signed, but not yet ratified the treaty; see Alston 1990; Felice 2010, pp. 233–256.

[4] See for more details Ssenyonjo 2009, pp. 203–243.

- the right to an adequate standard of living, including the rights to food, clothing and housing (Article 11 ICESCR); and
- the right to health (Article 12 ICESCR).[5]

The *Committee on Economic, Social and Cultural Rights* (CESCR),[6] established by the *United Nations Economic and Social Council* (ECOSOC), has successively elaborated so-called *General Comments* on these rights, shaping further the content of the obligations arising therefrom.[7] Chapter 3 will discuss this issue in greater detail. The *General Comments* do not have direct legal effect, but their importance must not be underestimated: So far they represent the most important source for the interpretation of the Covenant and are therefore commonly used in the academic literature as a starting point for continuing analysis.

However, the central task of the CESCR is the monitoring of the implementation reports on the Covenant, which must be submitted by the States Parties periodically.[8] Every 5 years, national governments must demonstrate the progress that has been made in the implementation of the obligations of the Covenant and the challenges which confront them in this process. Non-governmental organizations (NGOs) also have the opportunity to present their opinion on the situation by submitting so-called "shadow reports" to the CESCR; they are of particular value to the Committee in those cases where governments themselves do not entirely fulfil their reporting obligations (for example, by simply repeating legal texts without making any reference to the relevant facts). Based on this information, a working group of the CESCR firstly issues written questions to the respective government on the implementation of the rights of the Covenant. The CESCR then discusses the social rights situation of the country with government representatives in a public hearing, and prepares *Concluding Observations*, explicitly stating concrete breaches of the Covenant obligations where applicable, but also proposing ways to approach the problems effectively. In its next country report, the government must be responsive again to the suggestions of the CESCR, and explain the measures it has taken to improve the human rights situation in the concrete criticized cases. The country report procedure has some political impact, especially because the *Concluding Observations* are made public, but many consider it insufficiently effective, as the Committee can only apply weak pressure in cases where a State is not willing

---

[5] For another systematization see, for example, Pollmann and Lohmann 2012, who differentiate between subsistence rights (inter alia the rights to an adequate standard of living, to food, clothing and housing, and the right to health) and social rights (the right to social security and the protection of the family).

[6] ECOSOC Resolution 1985/17, 28.5.1985. For an analysis of the work of the CESCR see Langford and King 2008; Odello and Seatzu 2013, pp. 108–291.

[7] www2.ohchr.org/english/bodies/cescr/comments.htm; cf also Tomuschat 2010, pp. 190–191; Riedel 2010, paras 11–14.

[8] See Kälin and Künzli 2009, pp. 211–218; for an analysis of these reports—mainly with respect to Articles 9 and 11 ICESCR—see Davy 2013.

to cooperate.[9] In addition, the procedure implies considerable bureaucratic effort, especially for poorer developing countries—a factor that should not be neglected, especially when taking into account that many other international treaties provide for equivalent reporting obligations.[10]

Not long ago, the monitoring system of the ICESCR was developed further: In 2008, the *UN General Assembly* adopted an *Optional Protocol* to the ICESCR (OP),[11] stipulating in Articles 1–9 an individual complaints procedure.[12] Accordingly, not only those affected directly by human rights violations have the opportunity to file a complaint with the CESCR, but also trade unions or NGOs, for example. The notification to the CESCR must be submitted within one year of the exhaustion of domestic legal remedies. The introduction of this individual complaints procedure should eventually mitigate the recurrent allegations of justiciability deficiencies against social human rights.[13] According to Article 11(2) OP, the CESCR may, on receipt of relevant information about "grave or systematic" violations of social rights by a State Party, initiate its own investigations on the human rights situation in the country. Again, it can gather (even anonymously, as the case may be) evidence from NGOs or from victims of human rights violations, but, in contrast to the individual complaints procedure, is not obliged to wait for the outcome of the domestic court procedure.[14] Furthermore, Article 10 OP stipulates the procedure of so-called inter-State communications, which will presumably not be of much practical relevance as governments usually refrain from denouncing the social injustices of other States.

---

[9] Kälin and Künzli 2009, pp. 217–218, however, rightly point to the fact that the criticism of the lack of effectiveness of the procedure mostly misses the point: "(T)he awareness-raising potential of the process of preparing a country report should not be underestimated, provided, of course, that all relevant administrative bodies are involved and civil society is genuinely given a say. … At the same time, the consensus-based procedure enables the committees not only to denounce treaty violations but also to identify ways of tackling them and to commend positive elements".

[10] There is obviously a need for streamlining these manifold reporting obligations; see Kälin and Künzli 2009, pp. 218–220.

[11] UN Doc. A/RES/63/435, 5.3.2009; https://treaties.un.org/Pages/ViewDetails.aspx?src=TREATY&mtdsg_no=IV-3-a&chapter=4&lang=en; see Tomuschat 2005; Mahon 2008; de Albuquerque 2010; Vandenbogaerde and Vandenhole 2010; Grote 2012; Riedel et al 2014, pp. 28–35.

[12] For a comparison of the OP with the procedures of the ACHPR see Chenwi 2012, pp. 244–256.

[13] It is confirmed that this perception cannot be maintained nowadays, especially by national law: Social rights have been explicitly included in the catalogue of basic rights in many constitutions and are the subject of court proceedings (see infra Sect. 3.1. footnote 7); for the ICESCR see Schrijver 2013, p. 150: "It is a widespread misunderstanding that the rights contained in this Covenant are merely programmatory and hence not capable of direct application and non-justiciable, as opposed to those contained in the ICCPR." Cf. also, generally on this debate, Dennis and Stewart 2004, p. 515; Schneider 2004, pp. 24–34; Shany 2007; Ssenyonjo 2009, pp. 5, 12; Whelan and Donnelly 2007, pp. 932–936; Riedel 2008; Osiatynski 2009, pp. 116–126; Gearty and Mantouvalou 2011; Freeman 2011, p. 181; McBeth et al. 2011, pp. 29–32; Eichenhofer 2012, pp. 203–206; Krennerich 2013, pp. 116–123; Mahler 2013.

[14] Vedder 2009, para 152.

2.2 Social Rights Obligations in Special Human Rights Treaties

Social rights are not only covered by the ICESCR, but are also protected by various other treaties adopted on an international level for the protection of human rights. The *Convention on the Elimination of All Forms of Discrimination against Women* (CEDAW),[15] the *Convention on the Rights of the Child* (CRC),[16] the *International Convention on the Protection of the Rights of All Migrant Workers and Members of Their Families* (CMW)[17] and the *Convention on the Rights of Persons with Disabilities* (CRPD)[18] all contain the right to health[19] as well as the right to social security.[20] The right to an adequate standard of living is not included in the CMW; however, it is part of the other three special human rights instruments.[21] Alongside the country report procedure, which is obligatory for all contracting parties, all these conventions provide for optional individual complaint procedures. These procedures are under the responsibility of separate committees which are established under the respective treaty and are staffed with independent experts.[22] Beyond that, the *Open-Ended Working Group on Ageing*,[23] established by the *General Assembly*, deals with the question whether additional special international protection in favour of elderly people should be provided. In particular, both the Group of Latin America and Caribbean Countries and also many NGOs[24] support the drafting of a new convention, while other groups of States are more reluctant with regard to this issue.[25]

---

[15] 1249 UNTS 13, https://treaties.un.org/Pages/ViewDetails.aspx?src=TREATY&mtdsg_no=IV-8&chapter=4&lang=en; see, generally, on the social rights of women Barak-Erez 2007; van Leeuwen 2010; Fredman 2013; Chinkin 2014.

[16] 1577 UNTS 3; https://treaties.un.org/Pages/ViewDetails.aspx?src=TREATY&mtdsg_no=IV-11&chapter=4&lang=en; see Khadka 2013; Nolan 2013.

[17] 2220 UNTS 3; https://treaties.un.org/Pages/ViewDetails.aspx?src=TREATY&mtdsg_no=IV-13&chapter=4&lang=en.

[18] 2515 UNTS 3; https://treaties.un.org/Pages/ViewDetails.aspx?src=TREATY&mtdsg_no=IV-15&chapter=4&lang=en; see Ziv 2007.

[19] Articles 11(1)f, 12, 14(2)b CEDAW, Article 24 CRC, Articles 28, 43(1)e CMW, Article 25 CRPD.

[20] Articles 11(1)e, 14(2)c CEDAW, Article 26 CRC, Article 27 CMW, Article 28(2) CRPD.

[21] Article 14(2)h CEDAW, Article 27 CRC, Article 28(1)CRPD.

[22] *Committee on the Elimination of Discrimination Against Women*, http://www.ohchr.org/en/hrbodies/cedaw/pages/cedawindex.aspx; *Committee on the Rights of the Child*, http://www.ohchr.org/EN/HRBodies/CRC/Pages/CRCIndex.aspx; *Committee on Migrant Workers*, http://www.ohchr.org/EN/HRBodies/CMW/Pages/CMWIndex.aspx; *Committee on the Rights of Persons with Disabilities*, http://www.ohchr.org/en/hrbodies/crpd/pages/crpdindex.aspx.

[23] UN Doc. A/RES/65/182, 21.12.2010, see http://www.ohchr.org/EN/Issues/OlderPersons/Pages/OEWorkingGroup.aspx.

[24] http://www.rightsofolderpeople.org/; see also HelpAge 2011.

[25] See, for example, Open-ended Working Group on Ageing for the purpose of strengthening the protection of the human rights of older persons, 5th working session, 30.7.-1.8.2014, Opening statement by the European Union, http://social.un.org/ageing-working-group/documents/fifth/

From the very beginning, the *International Labour Organization* (ILO) has paid special attention to social rights. By drafting international conventions, the organization endeavours to globally enhance legal standards on the protection of the working population. Certainly, the main focus of its mandate is the right to work and to fair working conditions, but the organization is also concerned with social rights, insofar as they refer to the working environment. The central treaty document that has been submitted by the ILO is the *Social Security (Minimal Standards) Convention No. 102* of 1952.[26] It covers all relevant social risks (illness, unemployment, age, work accidents and occupational diseases, etc.), but the contracting parties commit themselves to guarantee social protection only to a certain proportion of the population.[27] However, the obligations arising from ratification of the Convention are quite extensive, with the result that only a rather small number of States—so far 50 countries, among them the industrialized nations in particular—have yet agreed to undergo monitoring of social standards by the supervisory institutions of the ILO. Therefore, throughout recent years, the ILO has shifted its attention towards the further development of social security issues on the *soft law* level[28] (see below Sects. 2.5 and 4.3) and to the addressing of increasingly special problems that newly industrializing and developing countries face in this context. In particular, it tackles the problem that the vast majority of the working population in this part of the world belong to the informal sector of the economy and is therefore not covered by conventional social security systems. The first important result of this policy reorientation by the ILO was expressed in the adoption of the *Social Protection Floors Recommendation* by the *International Labour Conference* in 2012 (see in detail below Sect. 5.2). This recommendation, which has received almost unanimous support from the Member States of ILO, entails access to primary health care and sets minimum standards on income security for all citizens, while requesting governments to continuously raise basic coverage up to the level specified by existing ILO agreements.

2.3 The Protection of Social Rights by Charter-Based Bodies

While our focus has so far been on those institutions dealing with social rights on the basis of special human rights conventions, the following will give a brief overview of the activity of so-called Charter-based bodies. The *UN Charter* itself constitutes a fundamental pillar of global human rights protection: According to

(Footnote 25 continued)
European%20Union_Opening%20Statement.pdf; see, generally, on the (social) protection of older persons Mégret 2011; Leisering 2011.

26 210 UNTS 131; http://www.ilo.org/dyn/normlex/en/f?p=NORMLEXPUB:12100:0::NO::p12100_instrument_id:312247; see also infra Sect. 4.3.

27 See Nussberger 2005, p. 126.

28 See infra Sects. 2.5, 4.3 and 5.2.

Article 55 UN, the *United Nations* as a whole is bound to foster "universal respect for, and observance of, human rights and fundamental freedoms without distinction as to race, sex, language, or religion". Individual Member States, on the other hand, are committed "to take joint and separate action in cooperation with the Organization for the achievement of the purposes set forth in Article 55", according to Article 56 UN. Further specifications on these two fundamental normative principles are not stipulated in the Charter itself; instead, they were made in its aftermath by the adoption of the UDHR in 1948, both Covenants on Human Rights in 1966[29] and a multitude of additional special conventions. In this context it is worth noting that, for example, the CESCR (see supra Sect. 1.1) has been incorporated on the basis of the *UN Charter*. Thus, in contrast to the other human rights conventions of the UN, no distinct body is responsible for the monitoring of the ICESCR, but ECOSOC—one of the principal organs of the UN—has taken over the task of incorporating the relevant committee of experts.[30] Its members are therefore not elected by the Signatory States of the ICESCR, but by members of ECOSOC.

The central (and probably best known to the public) UN organ dealing with the implementation of global human rights standards is the *Human Rights Council* (HRC)[31] which succeeded the *United Nations Commission on Human Rights* (UNCHR) in 2006. It is a subsidiary body to the *UN General Assembly* and is comprised of representatives of 47 Member States divided into regional groups. Located in Geneva, the HRC's task is to promote general respect for human rights protection and it is primarily concerned with severe and systematic human rights violations and issuing recommendations with respect to these.[32] In addition, it is charged with the coordination and continuous integration of human rights issues in all areas within the UN system. It is explicitly stated in its founding document that the HRC shall protect the principle of universality of human rights, hence addressing *all* human rights in its work.[33] For example, within the newly introduced general reporting mechanism to be regularly put into practice by each UN Member State (the so-called *Universal*

[29] Together with the UN Charter and the UDHR, these two covenants form the so-called "International Bill of Rights".

[30] Cf. Tomuschat 2010, p. 172.

[31] http://www.ohchr.org/EN/HRBodies/HRC/Pages/HRCIndex.aspx. In addition the *Office of the High Commissioner for Human Rights* (OHCHR) is to be mentioned, whose task is to support the work of the UN human rights mechanisms and to coordinate UN human rights education and public information activities; http://www.ohchr.org/EN/AboutUs/Pages/WhoWeAre.aspx.

[32] It can also schedule theme-orientated meetings on current global human rights issues. Examples with a particular focus on social rights are the 7th special session on "The negative impact on the realization of the right to food of the worsening of the world food crisis, caused inter alia by the soaring food prices" in 2008, http://www.ohchr.org/EN/HRBodies/HRC/SpecialSessions/Session7/Pages/7thSpecialSession.aspx; and the 10th special session on "The Impact of the Global Economic and Financial Crises on the Universal Realization and Effective Enjoyment of Human Rights" in 2009, http://www.ohchr.org/EN/HRBodies/HRC/SpecialSessions/Session10/Pages/10thSpecialSession.aspx.

[33] UN Doc. A/RES/60/251, 15.3.2006, para 4.

Periodic Review, UPR),[34] the implementation of all international legal obligations concerning human rights—i.e. also social rights—is to be monitored. Initial experiences with this newly established tool already indicate that the HRC is indeed trying to meet its mission of respecting the principle of universality.

In addition to the complaints procedure (formerly known as the so-called "1503 Procedure") that can be initiated "to address consistent patterns of gross … violations of all human rights"[35] and the country mandates, the HCR has made use of further mechanisms in order to exercise its mandate. For example, it is empowered to appoint *Working Groups* and *Special Rapporteurs* or so-called *Independent Experts* to examine special issues in human rights protection.[36] Not only single rights, but also overarching issues are taken into consideration in the framework of these *Special Procedures*. Furthermore, the main criterion for the investigation mandate of the *Special Procedures* is not merely the treaties that the respective country has actually ratified, but the considerably broader human rights norms set down by the UDHR. In particular, the following *Special Procedures* are relevant within the context of social rights:

- Adequate housing (Leilani Farha)[37]
- Effects of foreign debt and other related international financial obligations of States on the full enjoyment of human rights particularly economic, social and cultural rights (Juan Pablo Bohoslavsky)[38]
- Right to food (Hilal Elver)[39]
- Right of everyone to the enjoyment of the highest attainable standard of physical and mental health (Danius Puras)[40]
- Enjoyment of all human rights by older persons (Rosa Kornfeld-Matte)[41]
- Right to safe drinking water and sanitation (Catarina de Albuquerque)[42]
- Extreme poverty and human rights (Philip Alston)[43]
- Rights of persons with disabilities[44]
- Human rights and international solidarity (Virginia Dandan).[45]

---

[34] http://www.ohchr.org/en/hrbodies/upr/pages/uprmain.aspx.

[35] Institution-building of the UN Human Rights Council, UN Doc. A/HRC/RES/5/1, 18.6.2007; for the procedure see in more detail Vedder 2009, paras 155–161.

[36] Rudolf 2000; Subedi 2011; see, with a special focus on economic, social and cultural rights, also Golay et al. 2011.

[37] http://www.ohchr.org/EN/Issues/Housing/Pages/HousingIndex.aspx.

[38] http://www.ohchr.org/EN/Issues/Development/IEDebt/Pages/IEDebtIndex.aspx.

[39] http://www.ohchr.org/EN/Issues/Food/Pages/FoodIndex.aspx.

[40] http://www.ohchr.org/EN/Issues/Health/Pages/SRRightHealthIndex.aspx.

[41] http://www.ohchr.org/EN/Issues/OlderPersons/IE/Pages/IEOlderPersons.aspx. The Special Rapporteur will be appointed at the 27th session of the HRC in September 2014.

[42] http://www.ohchr.org/EN/Issues/WaterAndSanitation/SRWater/Pages/SRWaterIndex.aspx.

[43] http://www.ohchr.org/EN/Issues/Poverty/Pages/SRExtremePovertyIndex.aspx.

[44] UN Doc. A/HRC/26/L.9, 20, 20.6.2014; http://daccess-dds-ny.un.org/doc/UNDOC/LTD/G14/057/27/PDF/G1405727.pdf?OpenElement.

[45] http://www.ohchr.org/EN/Issues/Solidarity/Pages/IESolidarityIndex.aspx.

Of special importance for the design of North-South relations—and consequently also for the consolidation of social rights in development cooperation—is the *Intergovernmental Working Group on the Right to Development*[46] founded in 1998 and supported by the *High-level Task Force* since 2004.[47] The work of both bodies is based on the *Declaration on the Right to Development* of 1986,[48] Article 6 (2) of which emphasizes the indivisibility and the mutual dependence of individual human rights and highlights, in several other parts, the importance of conventional human rights protection, including social rights (inter alia in its preamble, in Article 1[1], Article 2[2], Article 3[3], Article 5 und Article 9[2]). In 2005, the *High-level Task Force* was instructed to base its future work upon the eighth *Millennium Development Goal* (MDG 8), aiming to establish a "Global Partnership for Development",[49] and to develop criteria allowing for regular monitoring of global partnerships, with regard to the realization of the right to development.[50] The auditing standards developed on the basis of this mandate reveal, in the eyes of UN experts, the bridge-building function of the right to development in the relationship between human rights protection and the practice of development policy.[51] Alongside the main content, summarized firstly in a *core norm,*[52] the *Task Force* allocates three so-called *attributes* to the right to development: "comprehensive and human-centred development policy", "participatory human rights processes" and "social justice in development". The extent to which pre-existing development partnerships are directed towards these attributes and whether or not they are capable of realizing the core elements of the right to development shall be assessed using a wide-ranging catalogue of criteria, sub-criteria and indicators. The focus on development cooperation based on human rights, and adapted to the particular requirements of social rights, becomes evident in the distinctive position of criterion 1(a) "constant improvement in socio-economic well-being" (with its sub-criteria health, education, housing and water, work and social security, food security).

---

[46] The *Open-ended Working Group* was established on the basis of the Resolution 1998 of the UN Commission on Human Rights (E/CN.4/RES/1998/72); for previous activity of the *Working Group* see http://www.ohchr.org/EN/Issues/Development/Pages/WGRightToDevelopment.aspx.

[47] *High-level Task Force on the Implemen-tation of the Right to Development*, http://www.ohchr.org/EN/Issues/Development/Pages/HighLevelTaskForce.aspx; cf. also Salomon 2005; von Schorlemer 2008, pp. 215–216.

[48] UN Doc. A/RES/41/128, 4.12.1986.

[49] See for more information on MDG 8 http://www.un.org/millenniumgoals/global.shtml.

[50] UN Doc. E/CN.4/2005/25, 3.3.2005, para 54(i).

[51] See von Schorlemer 2008, p. 218; cf. also Aguirre 2008, pp. 92–93; for an overview of the current state of the debate on the right to development see Piovesan 2013; von Bernstorff 2014, pp. 93–96.

[52] "The right to development is the right of peoples and individuals to the constant improvement of their well-being and to a national and global enabling environment conducive to just, equitable, participatory and human-centred development respectful of all human rights." See for more details the Report of the High-Level Task Force on the implementation of the right to development on its sixth session—Addendum: Right to development criteria and operational sub-criteria, UN-Doc. A/HRC/15/WG.2/TF/2/Add.2., 8.3.2010.

The EU has rightly pointed to the fact that in this context great importance should be attached to the ratification and effective implementation of the core UN and ILO instruments.[53]

Since 2011, another working group has been concerned with the topic of "Human Rights and Transnational Corporations and other Business Enterprises".[54] Its task consists primarily in supporting the distribution and implementation of the *UN Guiding Principles on Business and Human Rights* and in fostering the respect of social rights in this context.[55] Related questions will be discussed in greater detail further below (see Sect. 3.2). An additional intergovernmental working group dealing primarily with social rights has joined recently in 2012: Its mandate is to negotiate, finalize and submit a draft UN declaration on the rights of peasants and other people working in rural areas.[56]

2.4 Regional Human Rights Instruments in Developing Countries

The *American Convention on Human Rights* of 1969[57] is the oldest, non-European human rights treaty to have been concluded at a regional level. It entails only a few vague stipulations with regard to social rights,[58] but it is the basis of an additional protocol from 1988: the so-called *San Salvador Protocol*[59] which contains most of the conventional social rights, such as the right to social security, the right to health and to a healthy environment as well as the right to food (but not the right to adequate living conditions, as stipulated in the ICESCR). In addition, special guarantees to protect certain groups (children, elderly and handicapped people) have been included in the protocol. It stipulates a country report procedure as a

[53] EU Contribution on the Right to Development, 16.4.2012, http://www.ohchr.org/Documents/Issues/Development/Session13/EUSubmission.pdf.

[54] http://www.ohchr.org/EN/Issues/Business/Pages/WGHRandtransnationalcorporationsandotherbusiness.aspx.

[55] See infra Sect. 3.2.

[56] http://www.ohchr.org/EN/HRBodies/HRC/RuralAreas/Pages/WGRuralAreasIndex.aspx.

[57] OAS Treaty Series No. 36; 1144 UNTS; https://treaties.un.org/doc/Publication/UNTS/Volume%201144/volume-1144-I-17955-English.pdf.

[58] See, for example, Article 26: "The States Parties undertake to adopt measures, both internally and through international cooperation, especially those of an economic and technical nature, with a view to achieving progressively, by legislation or other appropriate means, the full realization of the rights implicit in the economic, social, educational, scientific, and cultural standards set forth in the Charter of the Organization of American States as amended by the Protocol of Buenos Aires".

[59] *Additional Protocol to the American Convention on Human Rights in the area of Economic, Social, and Cultural Rights*, OAS Treaty Series No. 69; http://www.oas.org/juridico/english/treaties/a-52.html; see Gómez 2007, pp. 171–174; Ruiz Chiriboga 2013.

review mechanism. Additionally, the *Inter-American Commission on Human Rights* (IACHR)[60] may engage in the implementation of the protocol in the Member States and issue corresponding recommendations.[61] The protocol entered into force in 1999, but was only ratified by 16 out of a total 24 Member States. It is, furthermore, worth mentioning the *Inter-American Convention on the Elimination of All Forms of Discrimination against Persons with Disabilities* from 1999,[62] which also refers to the social rights of persons with disabilities, as well as the *San José Charter on the Rights of Older Persons in Latin America and the Caribbean* from 2012[63]—the first international legal document to focus on the social rights of elderly people in particular.

In Africa, the main human rights document is the *African Charter on Human and Peoples' Rights* from 1981[64] (the so-called *Banjul Charter*). Following the will of its authors, it reflects the African concept of human rights which is expressed, inter alia, by emphasizing group rights (such as the right to development) and by referring to solidarity obligations towards society.[65] In contrast to what is stipulated in the American and European "model", the Charter entails both civil and political rights, as well as economic, social and cultural rights. The social rights, however, are subject to some remarkable exemptions: The right to health and the right to education are guaranteed, whereas the right to social security and the right to an adequate standard of living—which is the very right in the catalogue of the ICESCR that includes, inter alia, the right to food (see below Sect. 4.1)—are not specified in the Charter. Nonetheless, the *African Commission on Human and Peoples' Rights* (ACHPR)[66] has given the Charter a broad interpretation. For example, in the *Ogoni case* in 2001, it was clarified that the rights to life, health and development stipulated in the Charter implicitly guarantee the right to food.[67]

60 http://www.oas.org/en/iachr/; see Melish 2009; cf. for an analysis of the jurisprudence of the *Inter-American Court on Human Rights* Tinta 2007; see also, generally, Seibert-Fohr 2008.

61 Article 19(7) *San Salvador Protocol.*

62 AG/RES 1608, http://www.oas.org/juridico/english/treaties/a-65.html.

63 LC/G.2537, http://www.cepal.org/celade/noticias/paginas/9/44929/CR_Carta_ENG.pdf.

64 1520 UNTS 217, https://treaties.un.org/doc/Publication/UNTS/Volume%201520/volume-1520-I-26363-English.pdf.

65 Naldi 2008, pp. 29–30 (with further references).

66 http://www.achpr.org/; see Mbazira 2006, pp. 342–353; Baderin 2007; Affa'a Mindzie 2008; Ssenyonjo 2011; Alemahu Yeshanew 2011.

67 *Social and Economic Rights Action Centre (SERAC) v. Nigeria* (2001), Communication No. 155/96, para 65; see also para 7 of the *Pretoria Declaration on Economic, Social and Cultural Rights in Africa*, adopted by the ACHPR in December 2004, http://www.achpr.org/instruments/pretoria-declaration/; and para 68 of the *Principles and Guidelines on the Interpretation of Economic, Social and Cultural Rights in the African Charter on Human and Peoples' Rights*, adopted by the ACHPR in November 2010, http://www.achpr.org/files/instruments/economic-social-cultural/achpr_instr_guide_draft_esc_rights_eng.pdf (for a similar approach with regard to the rights to housing, to water and sanitation and to social security see paras 77, 88 and 87 of this document); cf. furthermore Nwobike 2005; Chirwa 2009, pp. 324–325, 331–332.

Furthermore, social human rights for certain groups in Africa are guaranteed by the *African Charter on the Rights and Welfare of the Child* from 1990[68] and by the *Protocol to the African Charter on Human and Peoples' Rights on the Rights of Women in Africa* (the so-called *Maputo Protocol*) of 2003.[69]

In the Arab world, the *Arab Charter on Human Rights*[70] has been applicable law since 2008 and places signatory States under an obligation to respect all important social rights. The Asia-Pacific region, however, is the only part of the world in which no regional human rights treaties yet exist. Although the ASEAN group adopted the *ASEAN Human Rights Declaration* in 2012,[71] making comprehensive reference to social rights, this document has merely the status of *soft law*. In addition, representatives of civil society have criticized the document for allowing governments too many restrictions of the human rights guarantees contained therein, for example the very broad exemption clause in Article 7, according to which

> the realization of human rights must be considered in the regional and national context bearing in mind different political, economic, legal, social, cultural, historical and religious backgrounds.[72]

The *ASEAN Human Rights Declaration* does not provide for autonomous regional institutions to implement and control stipulated material obligations, but merely obliges Member States to cooperate on national, regional and international levels to protect and promote human rights.[73] Although institutions which are exclusively mandated to deal with human rights also exist in the region, namely the *ASEAN Intergovernmental Commission on Human Rights* (AICHR)[74] and the *ASEAN Commission on the Promotion and Protection of the Rights of Women and Children* (ACWC),[75] formalized complaints procedures for victims of human rights violations are not available, contrary to comparable human rights institutions in Africa, Latin America or Europe. Rather, the main task of both institutions is to offer advisory services to ASEAN Member States (inter alia through capacity-building

---

[68] OAU Doc. CAB/LEG/24.9/49, 11.7.1990; http://www.au.int/en/sites/default/files/Charter_En_African_Charter_on_the_Rights_and_Wlefare_of_the_Child_AddisAbaba_July1990.pdf; cf. Viljoen 1998; Peter and Mwalimu 2012; Imoh and Ansell 2014.

[69] OAU Doc. CAB/LEG/66.6, 13.9.2000); http://www.achpr.org/files/instruments/women-protocol/achpr_instr_proto_women_eng.pdf; see Banda 2008; Mayanja 2012.

[70] Published in International Human Rights Reports 12 (2005), p. 893; see Rishmawi 2010.

[71] http://www.asean.org/news/asean-statement-communiques/item/asean-human-rights-declaration.

[72] On criticism of this provision cf. Shanahan Renshaw 2013, p. 568. Generally on the debate on Asian values in the international human rights discourse see Frick 2013, pp. 21–24.

[73] Article 39 *ASEAN Human Rights Declaration*.

[74] http://www.asean.org/communities/asean-political-security-community/category/asean-intergovernmental-commission-on-human-rights-aichr.

[75] http://www.asean.org/communities/asean-socio-cultural-community/category/acwc.

measures on the implementation of international human rights obligations), and to support the protection and promotion of human rights in the region through research, information and dialogue with civil society.[76] In this regard, their tasks are rather comparable to those of national human rights institutions.

2.5 Social Rights and International Soft Law

The human rights conventions discussed above are, on both the global and the regional levels, international law binding for all Contracting States, hence forming so-called *hard law*; if a State that has ratified one of these treaties infringes single obligations contained therein, its behaviour is considered to violate international law. Thereby, its binding status does not depend on the political feasibility or legal enforceability of the contractual obligations. As such, the social rights included in the ICESCR are *hard law*, despite the fact that so far, only a small number of Contracting States can be "accused" on the grounds of the *Optional Protocol* of violating social rights, either directly by their own citizens or by other governments (see supra Sect. 2.1).

One needs to distinguish *hard law* from international *soft law*, which is gaining significance as an important instrument in current international relations.[77] Resolutions of the UN and other international organizations,[78] bilateral political memoranda of understanding and codes of conduct, which are mainly directed towards transnational companies and are mostly prepared by international economic organizations (see Sect. 3.2), cannot be allocated to the catalogue of formal sources of international law. Even though a *numerus clausus* of formal sources of international law (as it might be stated in Article 38[1]ICJ) has been rejected by numerous law scholars,[79] State representatives and international law experts in the Third World, despite efforts for decades, have not succeeded in safeguarding a permanent position for UN GA Resolutions and Declarations in the catalogue of international *hard*

---

[76] *Terms of Reference of AICHR*, para 4; *Rules of Procedure of the ACWC;* http://www.asean.org/images/2012/Social_cultural/ACWC/documents/Rules%20of%20Procedure%20of%20ACWC_FINAL.pdf, paras 31, 48; *Terms of Reference of the ACWC;* http://www.asean.org/images/2012/Social_cultural/ACW/TOR-ACWC.pdf, paras 5.1–5.16.

[77] For a detailed discussion of international *soft law* see, inter alia, Bothe 1980; Heusel 1991; Fastenrath 1993; Hillgenberg 1999; Shelton 2003; Boyle and Chinkin 2007, pp. 211–229; Pauwelyn et al. 2012; Shaffer and Pollack 2013, pp. 197–222; Thürer 2009, paras 3, 25–32; the following section is based on Kaltenborn 1998, pp. 96–103.

[78] See, generally, Schermers and Blokker 2003, para 1141; with a special focus on the recommendations of ILO Leary 1997; Knauff 2010, pp. 275–279.

[79] Tomuschat 1976, p. 485; Bleckmann 1981, p. 338; van Hoof 1983, pp. 195–197; Hobe 1999, p. 264.

law norms.[80] Nevertheless, *soft law* norms[81] have an impact on the development of international law that should not be underestimated. It is, first and foremost, their task to contribute to the preparation of codification and also to the development of new customary international law[82]: The international community is increasingly struggling with the consensus-building necessary for the conclusion of new treaties, due to various international conflicts of interest; therefore States resort more and more frequently to the much more flexible instrument of *soft law*. Usually, before the process of negotiation and ratification of an international treaty is concluded or the creation of a norm of international customary law has been substantiated, many years have already passed, resulting in a precious loss of time with regard to a possibly urgent need for regulation. *Soft law* norms that do not require parliamentary approval or long-term State practice in order to become "effective" are therefore often much more suitable in a timely response to an international problem than formal sources of law.[83] In addition, *soft law* allows States involved in the norm-setting to agree on contents that go beyond a political minimum consensus. As an alternative form of regulation, it is rather targeted on acceptance than on enforcement; its supervision does not take place in court hearings, but in reporting obligations and equivalent monitoring mechanisms.[84]

Obviously, international *soft law* is by no means capable of replacing *hard law*, because its claim to regulate and to determine policy is much less distinct than in "classic" international law. *Soft law* norms cannot constitute any legally enforceable claims or prohibitions, as the parties participating in norm-setting are actually striving to avoid legal commitments.[85] It is, therefore, not surprising that some experts on international law have difficulties with the choice of terminology and refer to the inconsistency of the term *soft law*.[86] According to them, a stronger or

---

[80] The *Charter of Economic Rights and Duties of States* (UN-GA-Res. 3281 [XXIX],12.12.1974) has been discussed particularly intensely, as it should act—at least for the majority of UN members—as a legal basis for the "New International Economic Order"; cf., inter alia, Virally 1974; Tomuschat 1976.

[81] Until now, it is not clearly settled which elements are in particular attributed to *soft law*. The wide range of coverage of the term is described ostensively by Abbott and Snidal 2000, p. 422: "The realm of 'soft law' begins once legal arrangements are weakened along one or more of the dimensions of obligation, precision, and delegation. This softening can occur in varying degrees along each dimension and in different combinations across dimensions. We use the shorthand term *soft law* to distinguish this broad class of deviations from *hard law*—and, at the other extreme, from purely political arrangements in which legalization is largely absent." For a detailed presentation of various forms of *soft law* on the international level see Knauff 2010, pp. 258–296.

[82] Chinkin 2000, p. 31; Shelton 2014, pp. 161–162.

[83] Boyle 2010, p. 137; see also Riedel, 1986, p. 342; Engelhardt 2009, p. 504. In the field of social rights, the ILO is an important example of an organization that has recently opted, as a result of these strategic considerations, for an increased implementation of recommendations and codes of conduct instead of the conventional legislative form of draft conventions, see Abbott and Snidal 2000, p. 434; cf. on ILO legislative practice also Leary 1997.

[84] Knauff 2010, p. 256; see in this context also Benvenisti 2012; Corthaut et al. 2012.

[85] Aust 1986, p. 787; von Arnauld 2012, p. 112.

[86] Kokott 2005, p. 17; Heintschel von Heinegg 2014, p. 506; cf. also Thürer 2009, para 36.

weaker validity of law is not possible in legal logic.[87] Despite this critique, which is, of course, partially legitimate from the perspective of legal theory, it should not be overlooked that, meanwhile, the phenomenon of *soft law* has been firmly established on the international level and that a denial of its existence would be certainly out of touch with reality. For the international community, standard setting below the threshold of legally binding agreements has become an indispensable tool of policy making. In international relations, not only the legal binding force matters, but also the political or moral pressure that a norm may exert.[88] International law practice shows that resolutions and declarations are consulted as often as international treaties, in order to justify certain political positions.[89] The concern, initially raised by some observers, that an increasing practical importance of *soft law* norms could be accompanied by the destabilization of the international legal system,[90] has proved to be without merit. Besides its contribution to the creation of new, although (as yet) legally non-binding standards, *soft law* today rather assumes also stabilizing tasks such as the interpretation and concretization of already existing international law.[91] In this respect, *soft law* takes over complementary functions[92] and tasks of governance[93] within the international legal system, to the considerable benefit of, not least, the further development also of social human rights.

At the UN level, a multitude of politically significant, albeit legally "non-binding" declarations have been adopted within recent years, which are important milestones for the recognition and specification of social rights. Besides the already mentioned UDHR (see Sect. 2.1), only a few more examples shall be given here: The *Vienna Declaration of Human Rights* of 1993 acknowledges the interdependency and indivisibility of human rights.[94] This declaration, adopted by consensus, implied a considerable international valorisation for social rights in particular, as they were considered for decades to be rather second-rank in relation to civil

---

[87] Vitzthum 2013, para 152 (citing Thürer 1985, pp. 441 et seqq.); see also Klabbers 1996, p. 181: "Our binary law is well capable of handling all kinds of subtleties and sensitivities; within the binary mode, law can be more or less specific, more or less exact, more or less determinate, more or less wide in scope, more or less pressing, more or less serious, more or less far-reaching; the only thing it cannot be is more or less binding."

[88] Sepulveda 1990, p. 447; Knauff 2010, pp. 224–227; see also Kempen and Hillgruber 2012, p. 101.

[89] Pellet 1987, p. 127.

[90] Weil 1982, p. 423; cf. also d'Aspremont 2011, p. 222 and passim; d'Amato 2009, p. 899.

[91] Aust 1986, pp. 787–812; Riedel 1991, p. 83; Fastenrath 1993, p. 324.

[92] Bayne 2004, pp. 347–352; Thürer 2009, para 34.

[93] O'Connell 2003, p. 102; Knauff 2010, p. 250.

[94] Vienna Declaration and Programme of Action, UN World Conference on Human Rights, UN Doc. A/CONF.157/23, 25.6.1993, http://www.ohchr.org/en/professionalinterest/pages/vienna.aspx, para 5. See, generally, on the controversial issue of the indivisibility of human rights Petersmann 2003; Lohmann et al. 2005; Nickel 2008.

and political rights. Even though in some regions of the world—notably in the USA—this depreciation still exists in part,[95] the literature on international law agrees widely on the equal status of the rights laid down in both UN covenants.[96] Without a doubt, the Viennese *soft law* impulse has decisively influenced this development. The second important example is the *Millennium Declaration*, which demands "respect for all internationally recognized human rights" and "full protection and promotion … of civil, political, economic, social and cultural rights for all".[97] This Declaration has also been supported by all UN Member States; its impact in international law therefore reaches far beyond those of other global political documents. The final documents of other recent global conferences on development issues—latterly, for example, the *Doha Declaration on Financing for Development,*[98] the *Programme of Action for the Least Developed Countries for the Decade 2011–2020,*[99] the Outcome document of the *Fourth High Level Forum on Aid Effectiveness*[100] or the Outcome Document of the *UN Conference on Sustainable Development*[101]—often contain references to human rights, although mostly affirming norms already fixed in treaty law.

Referring to individual social rights, it turns out that the development of relevant *soft law* standards takes place predominantly within the human rights bodies[102] and specialized agencies of the UN. The *World Health Organization* (WHO), for example, makes repeated reference to the right to health in its resolutions,[103] whereas the *Food and Agriculture Organization* (FAO) is concerned with the

---

[95] Cf. Lewis 2009, 100; Albisa 2009, 176.

[96] See, for example, Bantekas and Oette 2013, p. 367: "… ESC rights are by no means the poor relative of civil and political rights. In fact many of the latter are meaningless without ESC rights."

[97] United Nations Millennium Declaration, UN-Doc. A/RES/55/2, 18.9.2000, http://www.un.org/millennium/declaration/ares552e.htm, paras 24, 25; see also infra Sect. 5.3.

[98] Final Declaration of the Follow-up International Conference on Financing for Development to Review the Implementation of the Monterrey Consensus, UN Doc. A/CONF.212/L.1/Rev.1, 9.12.2008, paras 2, 19; http://www.un.org/esa/ffd/doha/documents/Doha_Declaration_FFD.pdf .

[99] UN-Doc. A/CONF.219/3/Rev.1, https://www.un.org/wcm/webdav/site/ldc/shared/documents/IPoA.pdf, paras 26(i), 28(e), 29(e, f), 78.2(a, e), 89(b), 90.2(d), 129(a), 130(a).

[100] The Busan Partnership for Effective Development Co-operation, 1.12.2011, http://www.oecd.org/dac/effectiveness/49650173.pdf, paras 3, 11, 22.

[101] UN Doc. A/RES/66/288 ("The Future We Want"), 11.9.2012, paras 8, 9, 58(d), 108, 121, 138, 145, 152, 157, 229, 240, 241; http://daccess-dds-ny.un.org/doc/UNDOC/GEN/N11/476/10/PDF/N1147610.pdf?OpenElement.

[102] The *General Comments* of CESCR have already been mentioned (Sect. 2.1). They currently represent the most important *soft law* source in the field of social human rights.

[103] See, for example, in 2010–2012 WHA 63.16/2010, Annex 5, *WHO Global Code of Practice on the International Recruitment of Health Personnel* (para 3.4: "Member States should take into account the right to the highest attainable standard of health of the populations of source countries, …"); WHA 64.14/2011, Annex 4, *Global Health Sector Strategy on HIV/AIDS, 2011–2015* (para 100: "National HIV responses should implement and monitor policies and practices aimed at eliminating stigmatization, discrimination and other human rights abuses in health service delivery. … Links should be established with broader accountability mechanisms that assess progress in protecting human rights, including the right to health."); WHA 65.17/2012, Annex 4, *Global*

concretization of the right to food in its standards and guidelines.[104] The declarations of the ILO are of special importance for the right to social security; major examples from the recent past are the *Declaration on Social Justice for a Fair Globalization* adopted in 2008,[105] which declares the extension of social security to all humans (including the provision of a basic income for everyone) to one of the four strategic goals of the ILO, and the *Social Protection Floors Recommendation* of 2012.[106]

References

Abbott KW, Snidal D (2000) Hard and Soft Law in International Governance. Int Org 54:421–456

Affa'a Mindzie M (2008) The African Commission on Human and Peoples' Rights. In: Akokpari J, Zimbler DS (eds) Africa's human rights architecture. Fanele, Auckland Park, pp 204–232

Aguirre D (2008) The Human Right to Development in a Globalized World. Ashgate, Burlington

Albisa C (2009) Economic and Social Rights in the United States. Six Rights, One Premise. In: Soohoo C et al (eds) Bringing Human Rights Home: a History of Human Rights in the United States. University of Pennsylvania Press, Philadelphia, pp 173–197

Alemahu Yeshanew S (2011) Approaches to the justiciability of economic, social and cultural rights in the jurisprudence of the African Commission on Human and Peoples' Rights: Progress and perspectives. Afr Hum Rights L J 11:317–340

Alston Ph (1990) U.S. ratification of the Covenant on Economic, Social and Cultural Rights. The need for an entirely new strategy. AJIL 84:365–393

Aust A (1986) The Theory and Practice of Informal International Instruments. ICLQ 35:787–812

Baderin MA (2007) The African Commission on Human and Peoples' Rights and the Implementation of Economic, Social, and Cultural Rights in Africa. In: Baderin MA, McCorquodal R (eds) Economic, Social and Cultural Rights in Action. Oxford University Press, Oxford, pp 139–166

Banda F (2008) Protocol to the African Charter on the Rights of Women in Africa. In: Evans M, Murray R (eds) The African Charter on Human and Peoples' Rights. The system in practice 1986–2006, 2nd edn. Cambridge University Press, Cambridge, pp 441–474

Bantekas I, Oette L (2013) International Human Rights Law and Practice. Cambridge University Press, Cambridge

Barak-Erez D (2007) Social Rights as Womens's Rights. In: Barak-Erez D, Gross AM (eds) Exploring Social Rights. Between theory and practice. Hart, Oxford, pp 397–408

(Footnote 103 continued)
Vaccine Action Plan (para 2: "Immunization is, and should be recognized as, a core component of the human right to health …"); http://apps.who.int/gb/or/.

[104] See, for example, the *Voluntary Guidelines to support the progressive realization of the right to adequate food in the context of national food security*, adopted by the 127th Session of the FAO Council, 22.-27.11.2004; http://www.fao.org/docrep/meeting/009/y9825e/y9825e00.HTM (for an analysis of these guidelines see Engelhardt 2009, pp. 517–524); *Rome Principles for Sustainable Global Food Security*, 16.11.2009; http://www.fao.org/wsfs/wsfs-list-documents/en/.

[105] http://www.ilo.org/global/about-the-ilo/mission-and-objectives/WCMS_099766/lang–en/index.htm.

[106] See infra Sect. 5.2.

Bayne N (2004) Hard and Soft Law in International Institutions: Complements, Not Alternatives. In: Kirton JK, Trebilcock MJ (eds) Hard Choices, Soft Law. Voluntary Standards in Global Trade, Environment and Social Governance. Ashgate, Farnham, pp 347–352

Benvenisti E (2012) Toward a Typology of Informal International Lawmaking. Mechanisms and their Distinct Accountability Gaps. In: Pauwelyn J et al (eds) Informal International Lawmaking. Oxford University Press, Oxford, pp 297–309

Bleckmann A (1981) Die Funktionen der Lehre im Völkerrecht. Heymanns, Cologne

Bothe M (1980) Legal and Non-Legal Norms—A Meaningful Distinction in International Relations? NYIL 11:65–95

Boyle AE (2010) Soft law in International Lawmaking. In: Evans MD (ed) International Law, 3rd edn. Oxford University Press, Oxford, pp 122–140

Boyle AE, Chinkin ChM (2007) The Making of International Law. Oxford University Press, Oxford

Buergenthal Th (2007) Human Rights. In: Wolfrum R (ed) Max Planck Encyclopedia of Public International Law. Oxford University Press, Oxford. http://opil.ouplaw.com/view/10.1093/law:epil/9780199231690/law-9780199231690-e810?rskey=ioZ1FJ&result=1&prd=EPIL

Chenwi L (2012) An Appraisal of International Law Mechanisms for Litigating Socio-Economic Rights, with a Particular Focus on the Optional Protocol to the International Covenant on Economic, Social and Cultural Rights and the African Commission and Court. In: Liebenberg S, Quinot G (eds) Law and Poverty. Perspectives from South Africa and Beyond. Juta, Claremont, pp 241–263

Chinkin Ch (2000) Normative Development in the International Legal System. In: Shelton D (ed) Commitment and Compliance. The role of non-binding norms in the International Legal System. Oxford University Press, Oxford, pp 21–42

Chinkin Ch (2014) Gender and Economic, Social, and Cultural Rights. In: Riedel et al (eds) Economic, Social, and Cultural Rights in International Law. Contemporary Issues and Challenges. Oxford University Press, Oxford, pp 134–160

Chirwa DM (2009) African Regional Human Rights System. In: Langford M (ed) Social Rights Jurisprudence. Emerging Trends in International and Comparative Law. Cambridge University Press, Cambridge, pp 323–338

Corthaut T et al (2012) Operationalizing the Accountability of Informal International Lawmaking. In: Pauwelyn J et al (eds) Informal International Lawmaking. Oxford University Press, Oxford, pp 310–336

Crawford J (2012) Brownlie's principles of public International Law, 8th edn. Oxford University Press, Oxford

d'Amato A (2009) Softness in International Law. A Self-Serving Quest for New Legal Materials: a Reply to Jean d'Aspremont. EJIL 20:897–910

d'Aspremont J (2011) Formalism and the Sources of International Law. A Theory of the Ascertainment of Legal Rules. Oxford University Press, Oxford

Davy U (2013) Social citizenship going international: Changes in the reading of UN-sponsored economic and social rights. Int J Soc Welf 22(S1):15–31

de Albuquerque C (2010) Chronicle of an Announced Birth: The Coming into Life of the Optional Protocol to the International Covenant on Economic, Social and Cultural Rights. HRQ 32:144–178

Dennis MJ, Stewart DP (2004) Justiciability of economic, social, and cultural rights. Should there be an International complaints mechanism to adjudicate the rights to food, water, housing, and health? AJIL 98:462–515

Eichenhofer E (2012) Soziale Menschenrechte im Völker-, europäischen und deutschen Recht. Mohr Siebeck, Tübingen

Fastenrath U (1993) Relative Normativity in International Law. EJIL 4:305–340

Felice WF (2010) The Global New Deal. Economic and Social Human Rights in World Politics, 2nd edn. Rowman & Littlefield Publishers, Lanham

Fredman S (2013) Engendering socio-economic rights. In: Hellum A, Aasen HS (eds) Women's Human Rights: CEDAW in International, Regional and National Law. Cambridge University Press, Cambridge, pp 217–241
Freeman M (2011) Human Rights. An interdisciplinary approach, 2nd edn. Polity, Cambridge
Frick ML (2013) Universal Claim and Postcolonial Realities: The Deep Unease over Western-Centered Human Rights Standards in the Global South. In: Bagchi SS, Das A (eds) Human Rights and the Third World. Issues and Discourses. Lexington Books, Lanham, pp 17–30
Gearty CA, Mantouvalou V (2011) Debating Social Rights. Hart, Oxford
Golay Ch et al (2011) The Impact of the UN Special Procedures on the Development and Implementation of Economic, Social and Cultural Rights. Int J Hum Rights 15:299–318
Gómez V (2007) Economic, Social, and Cultural Rights in the Inter-American System. In: Baderin MA, McCorquodal R (eds) Economic, social and cultural rights in action. Oxford University Press, Oxford, pp 167–194
Grote R (2012) The Optional Protocol to the International Covenant on Economic, Social and Cultural Rights. Towards a more effective implementation of social rights? In: Hestermeyer H et al (eds) Coexistence, Cooperation and Solidarity. Liber amicorum Rüdiger Wolfrum. Nijhoff, Leiden, pp 417–436
Hannum H (1995) The Status of the Universal Declaration of Human Rights in National and International Law. Ga J Int Comp L 25:287–397
HelpAge (2011) Briefing paper for the first working session of the Open Ended Working Group on Ageing, April 18–21 2011. http://social.un.org/ageing-working-group/documents/HelpAge_briefing%20paper%20for%20the%201st%20session%20of%20the%20OEWG_%20April%202011.pdf
Heusel W (1991) "Weiches" Völkerrecht. Nomos, Baden-Baden
Hillgenberg H (1999) A Fresh Look at Soft Law. EJIL 10:499–515
Hobe St (1999) Die Zukunft des Völkerrechts im Zeitalter der Globalisierung. Perspektiven der Völkerrechtsentwicklung im 21. Jahrhundert. AVR 37:253–282
Imoh AT, Ansell N (eds) (2014) Children's lives in an era of children's rights. The progress of the Convention on the Rights of the Child in Africa. Routledge, Abingdon
Kälin W, Künzli J (2009) The Law of International Human Rights Protection. Oxford University Press, Oxford
Kaltenborn M (1998) Entwicklungsvölkerrecht und Neugestaltung der internationalen Ordnung. Rechtstheoretische und rechtspolitische Aspekte des Nord-Süd-Konflikts. Duncker & Humblot, Berlin
Kempen B, Hillgruber Ch (2012) Völkerrecht, 2nd edn. Beck, Munich
Khadka S (2013) Social rights and the United Nations-Child Rights Convention (UN-CRC). Is the CRC a help or hindrance for developing universal and egalitarian social policies for children's wellbeing in the "developing world"? Int J Child Rights 21:616–628
Klabbers J (1996) The Redundancy of Soft Law. NorJIL 65:167–182
Knauff M (2010) Der Regelungsverbund: Recht und Soft Law im Mehrebenensystem. Mohr Siebeck, Tübingen
Kokott J (2005) Soft Law Standards under Public International Law. A contribution on the Effects of the Transformation of International Law on the Sources of International Law. In: Nobel P (ed) International Standards and the law. Stämpfli Verlag, Bern, pp 15–41
Krennerich M (2013) Soziale Menschenrechte. Zwischen Recht und Politik. Wochenschau Verlag, Schwalbach
Langford M, King JA (2008) Committee on Economic, Social and Cultural Rights. In: Langford M (ed) Social Rights Jurisprudence. Emerging Trends in International and Comparative Law. Cambridge University Press, Cambridge, pp 477–516
Leary VA (1997) Nonbinding Accords in the Field of Labor. In: Brown Weiss E (ed) International compliance with nonbinding accords. American Society of International Law, Washington, pp 247–264
Leisering L ed (2011) Die Alten der Welt. Neue Wege der Alterssicherung im globalen Norden und Süden. Campus. Frankfurt a.M

Lewis H (2009) "New" Human Rights? U.S. ambivalence toward the international economic and social rights framework. In: Soohoo C et al (eds) Bringing Human Rights Home: a History of Human Rights in the United States. University of Pennsylvania Press, Philadelphia, pp 100–141
Lohmann G et al (2005) Die Menschenrechte: unteilbar und gleichgewichtig?. Universitäts-Verlag Potsdam, Potsdam
Mahler C (2013) Endlich gleichberechtigt—die Anerkennung der Justiziabilität von wirtschaftlichen, sozialen und kulturellen Rechten! In: Breuer M et al (eds) Der Staat im Recht. Festschrift für Eckart Klein. Duncker & Humblot, Berlin, pp 1189–1202
Mahon C (2008) Progress at the front: The draft Optional Protocol to the International Covenant on Economic, Social and Cultural Rights/Mahon. HRLR 8:617–646
Mayanja R (2012) The Protocol on the Rights of Women in Africa. In: Yusuf A (ed) The African Union. Legal and institutional framework: A manual on the Pan-African Organization. Nijhoff, Leiden, pp 455–476
Mbazira Ch (2006) Enforcing the economic, social and cultural rights in the African Charter on Human and Peoples' Rights. Twenty years of redundancy progression and significant strides. Afr Hum Rights L J 6:333–357
McBeth A et al (2011) The International Law of Human Rights. Oxford University Press, Oxford
Mégret F (2011) The Human Rights of Older Persons: A Growing Challenge. HRLR 11:37–66
Melish TJ (2009) The Inter-American Commission on Human Rights. In: Langford M (ed) Social Rights Jurisprudence. Emerging Trends in International and Comparative Law. Cambridge University Press, Cambridge, pp 339–371
Naldi GJ (2008) The African Union and the Regional Human Rights System. In: Evans M, Murray R (eds) The African Charter on Human and Peoples' Rights. The System in Practice 1986–2006, 2nd edn. Cambridge University Press, Cambridge, pp 20–48
Nickel JW (2008) Rethinking Indivisibility. Towards a theory of supporting relations between Human Rights. HRQ 30:984–1001
Nolan A (2013) Economic and social rights, budgets and the Convention on the Rights of the Child. Int J Child Rights 21:248–277
Nussberger A (2005) Sozialstandards im Völkerrecht. Eine Studie zu Entwicklung und Bedeutung der Normsetzung der Vereinten Nationen, der Internationalen Arbeitsorganisation und des Europarats zu Fragen des Sozialschutzes. Duncker & Humblot, Berlin
Nwobike JC (2005) The African Commission on Human and Peoples' Rights and the Demystification of Second and Third Generation Rights under the African Charter: Social and Economic Rights Action Center (SERAC) and the Center for Economic and Social Rights (CESR) v. Nigeria. Afr J Legal Stud 1:129–146
O'Connell ME (2003) The Role of Soft Law in a Global Order. In: Shelton D (ed) Commitment and compliance. The role of non-binding norms in the International Legal System. Oxford University Press, Oxford, pp 100–114
Odello M, Seatzu F (2013) The UN Committee on Economic, Social and Cultural Rights. The law, process and practice. Routledge, Abingdon
Osiatyński W (2009) Human rights and their limits. Cambridge University Press, Cambridge
Pauwelyn J et al (eds) (2012) Informal International Lawmaking. Oxford University Press, Oxford
Pellet A (1987) A New International Legal order: What Legal Tools for What Changes. In: Snyder F, Slinn P (eds) International Law of Development: Comparative Perspectives. Professional Books, Abingdon
Peter Ch M, Mwalimu UA (2012) The African Charter on the Rights and Welfare of the Child. In: Yusuf A (ed) The African Union. Legal and institutional framework: A manual on the Pan-African Organization. Nijhoff, Leiden, pp 477–493
Petersmann E-U (2003) On "indivisibility" of human rights. EJIL 14:381–385
Piovesan F (2013) The Right to Development from a Human Rights Approach: Conceptual Bases, Legal Framework, and Contemporary Challenges. In: Minkler L (ed) The State of Economic

and Social Human Rights. A Global Overview. Cambridge University Press, Cambridge, pp 306–328
Pollmann A, Lohmann G (eds) (2012) Menschenrechte. Ein interdisziplinäres Handbuch. J.B. Metzler, Stuttgart
Riedel E (1986) Theorie der Menschenrechtsstandards. Duncker & Humblot, Berlin
Riedel E (1991) Standards and Sources. Farewell to the Exclusivity of the Sources Triad in International Law? EJIL 2:58–84
Riedel E (2008) Zur Durchsetzung wirtschaftlicher, sozialer und kultureller Rechte im Völkerrecht. In: Giegerich Th, Zimmermann A (eds) Wirtschaftliche, soziale und kulturelle Rechte im globalen Zeitalter. Duncker & Humblot, Berlin, pp 71–93
Riedel E (2010) Committee on Economic, Social and Cultural Rights (CESCR). In: Wolfrum R (ed) Max Planck Encyclopedia of Public International Law. Oxford University Press, Oxford. http://opil.ouplaw.com/view/10.1093/law:epil/9780199231690/law-9780199231690-e765?rskey=KujFyG&result=1&prd=EPIL
Riedel E (2011) International Covenant on Economic, Social and Cultural Rights (1966). In: Wolfrum R (ed) Max Planck Encyclopedia of Public International Law. Oxford University Press, Oxford. http://opil.ouplaw.com/view/10.1093/law:epil/9780199231690/law-9780199231690-e836?rskey=KujFyG&result=4&prd=EPIL
Riedel E et al (2014) The Development of Economic, Social, and Cultural Rights in International Law. In: Riedel et al (eds) Economic, Social, and Cultural Rights in International Law. Contemporary Issues and Challenges. Oxford University Press, Oxford, pp 3–48
Rishmawi M (2010) The Arab Charter on Human Rights and the League of Arab States: an update. HRLR 10:169–178
Rudolf B (2000) Die thematischen Berichterstatter und Arbeitsgruppen der UN-Menschenrechtskommission. Springer, Berlin
Ruiz Chiriboga O (2013) The American Convention and the Protocol of San Salvador. Two Inter-Twined Treaties. NQHR 31:159–186
Salomon ME (2005) Towards a just institutional order. A commentary on the first session of the UN Task Force on the Right to Development. NQHR 23:409–438
Salomon ME (2013) Deprivation, Causation and the Law of International Cooperation. In: Langford M et al (eds) Global Justice, State Duties. The Extraterritorial Scope of Economic, Social, and Cultural Rights in International Law. Cambridge University Press, Cambridge, pp 259–296
Schermers HG, Blokker N (2003) International Institutional Law. Unity within Diversity, 4th edn. Nijhoff, Boston
Schneider J (2004) Die Justiziabilität wirtschaftlicher, sozialer und kultureller Menschenrechte. Deutsches Institut für Menschenrechte, Berlin
Schrijver N (2013) Approaching fifty: The Future of the International Covenant on Economic, Social and Cultural Rights. In: Hanschel D et al (eds) Mensch und Recht. Festschrift für Eibe Riedel. Duncker & Humblot, Berlin, pp 147–152
Seibert-Fohr A (2008) Wirtschaftliche, soziale und kulturelle Rechte in der Organisation Amerikanischer Staaten. In: Giegerich Th, Zimmermann A (eds) Wirtschaftliche, soziale und kulturelle Rechte im globalen Zeitalter. Duncker & Humblot, Berlin, pp 183–208
Sepulveda C (1990) Methods and Procedures for the Creation of Legal Norms in the International System of States: an Inquiry into the Progressive Development of International Law in the Present Era. GYIL 33:432–459
Shaffer G, Pollack ME (2013) Hard and Soft Law. In: Dunoff JL, Pollack M E(eds) Interdisciplinary Perspectives on International Law and International Relations: The State of the Article. Cambridge University Press, Cambridge, pp 197–222
Shanahan Renshaw C (2013) The ASEAN Human Rights Declaration 2012. HRLR 13:557–579

Shany Y (2007) Stuck in a moment in time: The international justiciability of economic, social and cultural rights. In: Barak-Erez D, Gross AM (eds) Exploring social rights. Between theory and practice. Hart, Oxford, pp 77–106
Shelton D (2003) Commitment and Compliance. The Role of Non-Binding Norms in the International Legal System. Oxford University Press, Oxford
Shelton D (2014) International Law and 'Relative Normativity'. In: Evans MD (ed) International Law, 4th edn. Oxford University Press, Oxford, pp 137–165
Ssenyonjo M (2009) Economic, Social and Cultural Rights in International Law. Hart, Oxford
Ssenyonjo M (2011) Economic, Social and Cultural Rights in the African Charter. In: Ssenyonjo M (ed) The African Regional Human Rights System. 30 Years after the African Charter on Human and Peoples' Rights. Brill, Leiden, pp 55–100
Subedi SP (2011) Protection of Human Rights through the Mechanism of UN Special Rapporteurs. HRQ 33:201–228
Thürer D (1985) "Soft Law"—eine neue Form des Völkerrechts? ZSchwR 104:429–453
Thürer D (2009) Soft Law. In: Wolfrum R (ed) Max Planck Encyclopedia of Public International Law. Oxford University Press, Oxford. http://opil.ouplaw.com/view/10.1093/law:epil/9780199231690/law-9780199231690-e1469?rskey=N6P2IK&result=7&prd=EPIL
Tinta MF (2007) Justicability of economic, social, and cultural rights in the inter-American system of protection of human rights. Beyond traditional paradigms and notions. HRQ 29:431–459
Tomuschat Ch (2005) An Optional Protocol for the International Covenant on Economic, Social and Cultural Rights. In: Dicke K et al (eds) Weltinnenrecht, Liber amicorum Jost Delbrück. Duncker & Humblot, Berlin, pp 815–834
Tomu-schat Ch (1976) Die Charta der wirtschaftlichen Rechte und Pflichten der Staaten. ZaöRV 36:444–491
Tomuschat Ch (2010) Human Rights. Between idealism and realism, 2nd edn. Oxford University Press, Oxford
van Hoof GJH (1983) Rethinking the Sources of International Law. Kluwer, Deventer
van Leeuwen F (2010) Women's Rights are Human Rights. The Practice of the United Nations Human Rights Committee and the Committee on Economic, Social and Cultural Rights. Intersentia, Antwerp
Vandenbogaerde A, Vandenhole W (2010) The Optional Protocol to the International Covenant on Economic, Social and Cultural Rights. An Ex Ante Assessment of its Effectiveness in Light of the Drafting Process. HRLR 10:207–237
Vedder Ch (2009) Die allgemeinen Menschenrechtspakte und ihre Verfahren. In: Merten D, Papier H-J (eds) Handbuch der Grundrechte in Deutschland und Europa, vol. VI/2: Europäische Grundrechte II—Universelle Menschenrechte. C.F. Müller, Heidelberg, para 174
Viljoen F (1998) Supra-national human rights instruments for the protection of children in Africa. The Convention on the Rights of the Child and the African Charter on the Rights and Welfare of the Child. Comp Int L J Southern Africa 31:199–212
Virally M (1974) La charte de droits et devoirs ecomoniques des Etats. AFDI 20:57–77
Vitzthum W Graf (2013) Begriff, Geschichte und Rechtsquellen des Völkerrechts. In: Vitzthum W Graf, Proelß A (eds) Völkerrecht, 6th edn. de Gruyter, Berlin, chapter 1
von Arnauld A (2012) Völkerrecht. C.F. Müller, Heidelberg
von Bernstorff J (2008) The Changing Fortunes of the Universal Declaration of Human Rights. Genesis and Symbolic Dimensions of the Turn to Rights in International Law. EJIL 19:903–924
von Bernstorff J (2014) Das Recht auf Entwicklung. In: Dann Ph et al (eds) Entwicklung und Recht. Nomos, Baden-Baden, pp 71–99
von Engelhardt M (2009) Opportunities and challenges of a soft law track to economic and social rights. The case of the voluntary guidelines on the right to food. VRÜ 42:502–527

von Heintschel Heinegg W (2014) Weitere Quellen des Völkerrechts. In: Ipsen K (ed) Völkerrecht. Ein Studienbuch, Beck, Munich, chapter 4

von Schorlemer S (2008) Das Recht auf Entwicklung. Recht des Individuums oder Recht der Völker? Vereinte Nationen 56:212–218

Weil P (1982) Vers une normativité relative en droit international. RGDIP 86:5–47

Whelan DJ, Donnelly J (2007) The West, economic and social rights, and the global human rights regime. Setting the record straight. HRQ 29:908–949

Ziv N (2007) The social rights of people with disabilities. Reconciling care and justice. In: Barak-Erez D, Gross AM (eds) Exploring social rights. Between theory and practice. Hart, Oxford, pp 369–395

Chapter 3
Social Rights Obligations—The Link Between Human Rights Law and International Development Law

Abstract The question of which concrete obligations arise from the protection of social rights leads in two directions: On the one hand, the content of the respective norms needs to be clarified—in which the specific content of individual rights (which will be discussed further under Sect. 3.4.) can be distinguished from general dimensions of obligations, which apply to all social rights in the same or similar manner (Sect. 3.1)—, on the other, the question of who is actually under an obligation to protect social rights. It is clear that States are committed by international law to comply with these laws, but it is more difficult to determine the status of obligation with respect to other actors: It is especially unclear if—and if it is the case, to which extent—multinational companies (Sect. 3.2) and international organizations working in the field of development cooperation are bound to comply with social rights (Sect. 3.4). Moreover, several questions still remain unanswered regarding the extraterritorial obligations of the States Parties to the ICESCR (Sect. 3.3). Since these extraterritorial obligations represent the link between Human Rights Law and International Development Law, they are (or at least should be) of special interest for those engaged in drafting the *Post 2015-Development Agenda*.

Keywords Obligations to respect, to protect and to fulfil · Violation of social rights · Principle of progressive realization · Minimum core obligations · Multinational companies · Extraterritorial obligations · Official development assistance · World Bank · World Trade Organization

3.1 The Tripartite Structure of Obligations and the Principle of Progressive Realization

In his study *Basic Rights* from 1980, the philosopher Henry Shue distinguishes between three dimensions of obligations arising from fundamental rights: negative obligations and positive obligations of protection as well as assistance.

M. Kaltenborn, *Social Rights and International Development*, SpringerBriefs in Law, DOI 10.1007/978-3-662-45352-0_3

> The complete fulfillment of each kind of right involves the performance of multiple kinds of duties. … (F)or every right to subsistence there are: I. Duties not to eliminate a person's only available means of subsistence – duties to *avoid* depriving. II. Duties to protect people against deprivation of the only available means of subsistence by other people – duties to *protect* from deprivation. III. Duties to provide for the subsistence of those unable to provide for their own – duties to *aid* the deprived.[1]

The typology developed by Shue has had significant influence, not only in political philosophy, but also in international legal jurisprudence[2] and among legal practitioners. The *Committee on Economic, Social and Cultural Rights* (CESCR), in particular, has succeeded in drawing, on the basis of the preliminary work in literature, a clear distinction between three different obligation levels for social rights. Thus, these rights are linked to obligations to respect, to protect and to fulfil.[3] Each of these dimensions of obligations can be specified for the individual rights and implemented into concrete legal norms. With regard to the right to food guaranteed in Article 11 ICESCR, for example, the *obligation to respect* requires the Member States not to take any measures preventing access to available food.[4] This means, for instance, that no land mines shall be laid in territories that are indispensable for the food supply of the local population; during humanitarian crisis situations, governments shall not inhibit food aid. A Contracting State satisfies its *obligation to protect* only if it ensures that access to food is not restricted by private persons or corporations. It must interfere, for example, where individual farmers or traders stockpile supplies in times of food shortage in order to bring them, priced at the rate of inflation, as the case may be, onto the market later. Finally, the *obligation to fulfil* requires the Contracting States to provide necessary food to their populations in the case of famine—or, if the States are not capable of doing so on their own, to seek appropriate assistance from the international community. Similar distinctions of several legal obligations can be drawn also for other social rights (see infra Sects. 3.1–3.3).

Regardless of the obligation category, a violation of social rights can be the result of either concrete State actions or failures to act in cases when action is necessary in principle. Following an invitation of the *International Commission of Jurists*, the *Urban Morgan Institute on Human Rights* (Cincinnati, Ohio) and the *Centre for Human Rights of the Faculty of Law of Maastricht University*, an expert commission has endeavored to specify the ICESCR rights and has, inter alia, compiled a catalogue of typical forms of violations:

> Violations of economic, social and cultural rights can occur through the direct action of States or other entities insufficiently regulated by States. Examples of such violations include: (a) the formal removal or suspension of legislation necessary for the continued enjoyment of an economic, social and cultural right that is currently enjoyed; (b) the active

---

[1] Shue 1996, pp. 52–53.

[2] Eide 1984, p. 154; van Hoof 1984, pp. 106–108; for a discussion of the different approaches see Sepúlveda 2003, pp. 161–173.

[3] Eide 2001, p. 23; cf. also Ssenyonjo 2009, pp. 23–26; De Schutter 2010, pp. 242–256.

[4] For this and the following cf. CESCR 1999a, Paras 15–20; Ziegler et al. 2011, pp. 18–20.

> denial of such rights to particular individuals or groups, whether through legislated or enforced discrimination; (c) the active support for measures adopted by third parties which are inconsistent with economic, social and cultural rights; (d) the adoption of legislation or policies which are manifestly incompatible with pre-existing legal obligations relating to these rights, unless it is done with the purpose and effect of increasing equality and improving the realization of economic, social and cultural rights for the most vulnerable groups; (e) the adoption of any deliberately retrogressive measure that reduces the extent to which any such right is guaranteed; (f) the calculated obstruction of, or halt to, the progressive realization of a right protected by the Covenant, unless the State is acting within a limitation permitted by the Covenant or it does so due to a lack of available resources or force majeure; (g) the reduction or diversion of specific public expenditure, when such reduction or diversion results in the non-enjoyment of such rights and is not accompanied by adequate measures to ensure minimum subsistence rights for everyone.[5] Violations of economic, social, cultural rights can also occur through the omission or failure of States to take necessary measures stemming from legal obligations. Examples of such violations include: (a) the failure to take appropriate steps as required under the Covenant; (b) the failure to reform or repeal legislation which is manifestly inconsistent with an obligation of the Covenant; (c) the failure to enforce legislation or put into effect policies designed to implement provisions of the Covenant; (d) the failure to regulate activities of individuals or groups so as to prevent them from violating economic, social and cultural rights; (e) the failure to utilize the maximum of available resources towards the full realization of the Covenant; …[6]

For each social right mentioned in the ICESCR, the *General Comments* edited by the CESCR list concrete examples which can be attributed to these different forms of action and omission. Further examples can be found in the jurisdiction of national courts, which have to apply social rights enshrined in the respective constitutions.[7] By means of comparative law, these rulings can be additionally consulted when the interpretation of international human rights guarantees is concerned.[8] It becomes clear, thus, that already a high degree of precision in the determination of social rights content has been attained. The old prejudice that

---

[5] Article 14 *Maastricht Guidelines on Violations of Economic, Social and Cultural Rights*, 22.–26.1.1997, http://www1.umn.edu/humanrts/instree/Maastrichtguidelines_.html.—All websites cited in this chapter have been last accessed 3 September 2014.

[6] Article 15 *Maastricht Guidelines on Violations of Economic, Social and Cultural Rights*.

[7] Provisions of national legislation and their control by constitutional courts are not subject of this study. On the enforcement of social rights in individual legal systems of the Global South cf. Coomans 2006; Gauri and Brinks 2008; Langford 2008; Bonilla Maldonado 2013; in particular on Latin American countries see Eckstein and Wickham-Crowley 2003; Courtis 2006; Ely Yamin 2006; Schilling-Vacaflor and Barrera 2011; on sub-Sahara Africa e.g. Mubangizi 2006; Ibe 2010; for an analysis of the comprehensive social rights jurisprudence particularly in South Africa see Bilchitz 2007, pp. 135–237; Mbazira 2009; Liebenberg 2010; Trilsch 2012, pp. 207–246 and passim; O'Connell 2012, pp. 48–77; Wilson and Dugard 2013; for the social rights jurisprudence of the *Supreme Court of India* see Kothari 2007; Shankar and Mehta 2008; O'Connell 2012, pp. 78–107; cf. in this context also, generally, Tushnet 2008; Landau 2012.

[8] See also Article 8 *Maastricht Guidelines on Violations of Economic, Social and Cultural Rights*: "… State practice and the application of legal norms to concrete cases and situations by international treaty monitoring bodies as well as by domestic courts have contributed to the development of universal minimum standards and the common understanding of the scope, nature and limitation of economic, social and cultural rights."

social rights are formulated too vaguely and therefore cannot be the basis of concrete, legally enforceable claims or obligations respectively,[9] can hence hardly be maintained nowadays. But obviously, the authors of ICESCR were also aware of the fact that hardly any State would be able to satisfy these obligations in full. As in other human rights documents, the ICESCR contains provisions that allow States to restrict the rights under certain conditions. For example, Article 4 stipulates that options on restrictions are available to States—yet within only a narrowly defined frame.[10] But one of the main features of human rights guaranteed on the ICESCR is primarily the fact that Contracting States are not obliged to guarantee these rights fully and immediately. Many States were indeed not able to do so, having regard to the economic and socio-political challenges related to it, and have, therefore, "only" agreed to the continuing improvement of existing standards and their implementation. According to the so-called principle of progressive realization, a Contracting State is bound

> to take steps … to the maximum of its available resources, with a view to achieving progressively the full realization of the rights recognized in the present Covenant by all appropriate means ….[11]

The Covenant hence differentiates between those States that can guarantee necessary social rights protection to their citizens due to their economic strength, and those that are not (yet) able to do so.

Right from the beginning, the CESCR has made intensive efforts to clarify the obligations that arise for the Contracting States of ICESCR from the principle of progressive realization. The *General Comment No. 3* from 1990[12] and another document on the same topic published in 2007[13] summarize the most important requirements that need to be taken into account when implementing social human rights against the background of the problem on resource scarcity as follows:

> The concept of progressive realization constitutes a recognition of the fact that full realization of all economic, social and cultural rights will generally not be able to be achieved in a short period of time. In this sense the obligation differs significantly from that contained in Article 2 of the International Covenant on Civil and Political Rights which embodies an immediate obligation to respect and ensure all of the relevant rights. Nevertheless, the fact that realization over time, or in other words progressively, is foreseen under the Covenant should not be misinterpreted as depriving the obligation of all meaningful content. It is on

[9] See for the debate on the justiciability of social rights the references supra Sect. 2.1, footnote 13.

[10] Most of the authors who have dealt in more detail with this provision also require, inter alia, that restrictions of social rights should be subject to a proportionality assessment; e.g. Müller 2009, pp. 583–584; Ssenyonjo 2009, p. 101; see also CESCR 2000, Para 29. Sometimes the provision is also interpreted in a way that restrictions cannot be justified by a lack of available resources; see McBeth et al. 2011, p. 164, Kradolfer 2012, p. 279; cf. on the relationship between Article 2(1) and Article 4 ICESCR also Alston and Quinn 1987, pp. 205–206.

[11] Article 2(1) ICESCR; see for an analysis of this principle Klee 2000, pp. 113–137; Sepúlveda 2003, pp. 174–184.

[12] CESCR 1990.

[13] CESCR 2007.

> the one hand a necessary flexibility device, reflecting the realities of the real world and the difficulties involved for any country in ensuring full realization of economic, social and cultural rights. On the other hand, the phrase must be read in the light of the overall objective, indeed the *raison d'être*, of the Covenant which is to establish clear obligations for States parties in respect of the full realization of the rights in question. It thus imposes an obligation to move as expeditiously and effectively as possible towards that goal. Moreover, any deliberately retrogressive measures in that regard would require the most careful consideration and would need to be fully justified by reference to the totality of the rights provided for in the Covenant and in the context of the full use of the maximum available resources.[14]

In their implementation of covenant obligations, the Contracting States possess a certain margin of appreciation; in particular, no obligation on the design of the economic and political system of a State can be drawn from the ICESCR:

> The Committee notes that the undertaking 'to take steps … by all appropriate means including particularly the adoption of legislative measures' neither requires nor precludes any particular form of government or economic system being used as the vehicle for the steps in question, provided only that it is democratic and that all human rights are thereby respected Thus, in terms of political and economic systems the Covenant is neutral and its principles cannot accurately be described as being predicated exclusively upon the need for, or the desirability of a socialist or a capitalist system, or a mixed, centrally planned, or laisser-faire economy, or upon any other particular approach.[15]

The States are also granted discretionary power to decide which measures are considered "appropriate" according to the covenant obligations. However, the CESCR has reserved the final judgment of the question for itself:

> … (T)he adoption of legislative measures, as specifically foreseen by the Covenant, is by no means exhaustive of the obligations of States parties. Rather, the phrase 'by all appropriate means' must be given its full and natural meaning. While each State party must decide for itself which means are the most appropriate under the circumstances with respect to each of the rights, the 'appropriateness' of the means chosen will not always be self-evident. It is therefore desirable that States parties' reports should indicate not only the measures that have been taken but also the basis on which they are considered to be the most 'appropriate' under the circumstances. However, the ultimate determination as to whether all appropriate measures have been taken remains one for the Committee to make.[16]

The respective economic starting position is certainly of utmost importance for the concrete range of obligations that have to be considered by States with regard to social human rights. Poorer developing countries, in particular, usually do not dispose of necessary resources to comply fully with the fulfilment obligations of the ICESCR.[17] This does not mean, however, that every obligation can be omitted, but requires a differentiated assessment of the specific resource investment:

---

[14] CESCR 1990, Para 9. For details of the prohibition of taking deliberately retrogressive measures see Sepúlveda 2003, pp. 323–332.

[15] CESCR 1990, Para 8.

[16] CESCR 1990, Para 4.

[17] See, generally, on the problem of lack of resources Alston and Goodman 2013, pp. 315–330.

> The 'availability of resources', although an important qualifier to the obligation to take steps, does not alter the immediacy of the obligation, nor can resource constraints alone justify inaction. Where the available resources are demonstrably inadequate, the obligation remains for a State party to ensure the widest possible enjoyment of economic, social and cultural rights under the prevailing circumstances. The Committee has already emphasized that, even in times of severe resource constraints, States parties must protect the most disadvantaged and marginalized members or groups of society by adopting relatively low-cost targeted programmes.[18] Should a State party use 'resource constraints' as an explanation for any retrogressive steps taken, the Committee would consider such information on a country-by-country basis in the light of objective criteria such as: (a) the country's level of development; (b) the severity of the alleged breach, in particular whether the situation concerned the enjoyment of the minimum core content of the Covenant; (c) the country's current economic situation, in particular whether the country was undergoing a period of economic recession; (d) the existence of other serious claims on the State party's limited resources; for example, resulting from a recent natural disaster or from recent internal or international armed conflict; (e) whether the State party had sought to identify low-cost options; and (f) whether the State party had sought cooperation and assistance or rejected offers of resources from the international community for the purposes of implementing the provisions of the Covenant without sufficient reason.[19]

This makes clear that the government of a poorer country cannot completely evade its responsibility: On the one hand, such States are under an explicit obligation to take at least the first steps, with foreign assistance if necessary, towards the gradual realization of social rights.[20] As States shall exploit *all* their potentialities, the pressure on governments to justify their decisions is very high when economic and socio-political priority-setting does not foresee the introduction or maintenance of measures aiming at poverty reduction and the realization of social rights. On the other hand, the CESCR in its *General Comment No. 3* has clearly stated that

> a minimum core obligation to ensure the satisfaction of, at the very least, minimum essential levels of each of the rights is incumbent upon every State party. Thus, for example, a State party in which any significant number of individuals is deprived of essential foodstuffs, of essential primary health care, of basic shelter and housing, or of the most basic forms of education is, *prima facie*, failing to discharge its obligations under the Covenant. If the Covenant were to be read in such a way as not to establish such a minimum core obligation, it would be largely deprived of its *raison d'être*. By the same token, it must be noted that any assessment as to whether a State has discharged its minimum core obligation must also take account of resource constraints applying within the country concerned Article 2(1) obligates each State party to take the necessary steps 'to the maximum of its available resources'. In order for a State party to be able to attribute its failure to meet at least its minimum core obligations to a lack of available resources it must demonstrate that every effort has been made to use all resources that are at its disposition in

---

[18] CESCR 2007, Para 4.

[19] CESCR 2007, Para 10. For an analysis of the term "maximum of available resources" see also Dowell-Jones 2004, pp. 44–51; Saul et al. 2014, pp. 143–151.

[20] CESCR 1990, Para 2: "... (W)hile the full realization of the relevant rights may be achieved progressively, steps towards that goal must be taken within a reasonably short time after the Covenant's entry into force for the States concerned Such steps should be deliberate, concrete and targeted as clearly as possible towards meeting the obligations recognized in the Covenant."

> an effort to satisfy, as a matter of priority, those minimum obligations.[21] The Committee wishes to emphasize, however, that even where the available resources are demonstrably inadequate, the obligation remains for a State party to strive to ensure the widest possible enjoyment of the relevant rights under the prevailing circumstances. Moreover, the obligations to monitor the extent of the realization, or more especially of the non-realization, of economic, social and cultural rights, and to devise strategies and programmes for their promotion, are not in any way eliminated as a result of resource constraints.[22]

The *General Comments* to the ICESCR contain information on the exact content of the minimum core obligations of the individual rights. It is striking that, besides the description on material minimum requirements to be implemented immediately, in each of these *General Comments* specific procedural guidelines are also formulated, such as the obligations to set up national action plans[23] or to take over monitoring tasks.[24] In addition, high priority is given to rules on non-discrimination.[25] Concerning material obligations, however, the *General Comments* do not provide for such precise targets, meaning that measureable standards on content for each individual case cannot be derived therefrom.[26] This is not surprising: Answering the question on which requirements are concretely—i.e. in a specific country at a specific point in time—applicable to the implementation of individual social human rights includes an extremely high degree of complexity, as the specific obligation content depends on numerous economic, political and socio-cultural factors in the respective countries.[27] There might be many situations in which it is not difficult to provide evidence that a State did not comply with ICESCR obligations because it clearly dropped below the "base line" arising out of the relevant

---

[21] CESCR 1990, Para 10. On the concept of (minimum) core obligations cf. also Brand and Russell 2002; Scheinin 2013.

[22] CESCR 1990, Para 11; cf. also CESCR 2001, Para 18: "… (B)ecause core obligations are non-derogable, they continue to exist in situations of conflict, emergency and natural disaster."

[23] CESCR 1992, Para 12; CESCR 1999a, Paras 21–23; CESCR 2003, Para 37(f); CESCR 2008, Para 59(d).

[24] CESCR 1992, Para 13; CESCR 1999a, Para 31; CESCR 2000, Para 43(f); CESCR 2003, Para 37(g); CESCR 2008, Para 59(f); cf. Ssenyonjo 2009, pp. 68–69.

[25] CESCR 1999a, Paras 18, 26; CESCR 2000, Para 43(a); CESCR 2003, Para 37(b); CESCR 2008, Para 59(b). On the relevance of the non-discrimination principle for the implementation of social rights obligations see CESCR 2009; Sepúlveda 2003, pp. 379–419; Ssenyonjo 2009, pp. 60, 85–97.

[26] See Sepúlveda 2003, p. 367: "Once it is established that states must guarantee a minimum essential level of each right, the question is to determine what constitutes the 'essential level' or 'core content' of each right. Over the years the Committee has struggled to identify the core content of each right, but has not met with much success. This is not to say that the Committee is to blame, because identifying the minimum entitlements without which a right loses its substance is a complex task and the results tend to be rather theoretical or abstract."

[27] Bantekas and Oette 2013, p. 378, rightly note that "… what remains unanswered is whether the minimalist approach associated with minimum core obligations presupposes differentiated standards between developed and developing countries." Some authors try to face this problem by supporting a country-specific *minimum threshold approach*; see, for example, Andreassen et al. 1988; for an examination of this issue in more depth see Bilchitz 2003; Young 2008.

minimum core obligations.[28] Often, however, one faces more complex circumstances that do not allow for such clear classification. Similar problems occur where wordings that were chosen in the *General Comments* to describe certain elements of the minimum core obligations remain (often inevitably) vague.[29] Against this background, scientific efforts to develop indicators or benchmarks[30] in order to reach further specification of obligations arising out of social rights should not be underestimated for the future role of social rights in the development discourse.

3.2 Social Rights and Multinational Corporations

When severe violations of social human rights in Third World countries are reported by the media, in many cases the predominant aspect of such reports is the activities of large, multinational corporations. There has always been a dichotomy in the role of such companies in the process of globalization: On the one hand, the private capital inflow via the investment activities of foreign enterprises is an indispensable part of economic development in newly industrializing and developing countries; in addition, there are numerous examples showing that the corporate culture of foreign investors can be a particular benchmark for the development of respective standards in the host country. On the other hand, recurrent cases of international companies acting irresponsibly towards their employees and the population living near the production site must not be overlooked. The unacceptable conditions in Bangladeshi textile factories that led to a number of spectacular accidents in 2013[31] are a particularly dramatic example of the socio-political "collateral damage" of a globalized economy. In fact, these events, reported extensively in the media, reflect just the tip of a giant iceberg: Many millions of people in Third World countries are involved directly or

---

[28] Cf. Bilchitz 2003, p. 12.

[29] According to CESCR 2003, Para 37(a) and (c), the obligation "(t)o ensure access to the minimum essential amount of water, that is sufficient and safe for personal and domestic uses to prevent disease" and "(t)o ensure physical access to water facilities or services that provide sufficient, safe and regular water" belongs to the *minimum core obligations* with relation to the right to water. These clauses—which can also be found in comparable form in other General Comments—include several indeterminate legal terms that can be interpreted differently depending on the respective regional and cultural context.

[30] For an overview on the application of indicators with regard to social human rights see Welling 2008; cf. also Manning 2009; Hunt and MacNaughton 2007; De Schutter 2010, pp. 479–512; Windfuhr 2013, pp. 362–363, 365–369; and, generally, Riegner 2014; on the special problems of measuring State compliance with the obligation to devote the "maximum of (their) available resources" (Article 2 [1] ICESCR) see Khalfan 2013, pp. 324–330; Sepúlveda 2003, pp. 316–319; Apodaca 2007; Corkery and Way 2012.

[31] New York Times, 24.4.2013 "Building Collapse in Bangladesh Leaves Scores Dead"; http://www.nytimes.com/2013/04/25/world/asia/bangladesh-building-collapse.html?pagewanted=all&module=Search&mabReward=relbias%3As%2C%7B%222%22%3A%22RI%3A15%22%7D.

indirectly in the production processes of internationally operating companies. They must content themselves with wages and working conditions that make a life with respect for basic social rights almost impossible.

The question of whether or not multinationals are considered legal entities, bound by international human rights norms, has been subject of lively discussions among practitioners and in the literature on international law. Until now, the view to grant them such legal status has not yet won majority support. However, the United States recognizes liability on the basis of the *Alien Tort Claims Act* (ATCA).[32] There, courts act on the assumption that international companies also bear responsibility as a matter of international law, in cases where they are either accused of international crimes or of participating in other human rights violations, which can be attributed in any way to a State at the same time (examples for such an attribution can be acts of incitement and abetment, or cooperation with government authorities as joint ventures[33]). Generally, on this basis, economic and social rights can hence be considered the basis of companies' tortious liability, such as the right to health in the harmful testing of non-licensed drugs,[34] or the right to freedom of association in case of violent persecution and intimidation of trade unionists.[35] However, the *US Supreme Court* made clear that it only recognizes liability under ATCA if the claim concerns infringements of fundamental norms in international law (e.g. the ban on torture, the prohibition of slavery, war crimes, crimes against humanity and, arguably, infringements of basic freedom rights such as the right to life).[36] Until now, there has been no indication that this strict position will be abandoned in the near future,[37] and in other countries, no approaches can currently be observed which go beyond the US treatment of liability.

In international law itself, the only efforts to extend human rights obligations to multinationals are being made on the level of *soft law*.[38] Besides the *ILO Tripartite Declaration of Principles Concerning Multinational Enterprises and Social Policy* of 1977[39] which referred to internationally recognized core labor standards, mention should be made of the *Guidelines for Multinational Enterprises*, enacted by the *Organization for European Co-operation and Development* (OECD) in 1976 and revised in 2000 and 2011.[40] Besides recommendations on compliance with certain

[32] 28 USC § 1350.

[33] Seibert-Fohr and Wolfrum 2005, pp. 166–177.

[34] *Abdullahi v. Pfizer*, 562 F.3d 163 (2d Cir. 2009), HLR 123 (2010), p. 768.

[35] *Sinaltrainal v. The Coca-Cola Co.*, No. 06-15851, 2009 WL 2431463 (11th Cir. 2009); HLR 123 (2009), p. 580.

[36] *Sosa v. Alvarez-Machain*, 542 U.S. 692 (2004); http://caselaw.lp.findlaw.com/scripts/getcase.pl?court=us&vol=542&invol=692.

[37] See e.g. *Kiobel v. Royal Dutch Petroleum Co.*, 133 S.Ct. 1659 (2013); HLR 127 (2013), p. 308.

[38] The following sections are based on Kaltenborn and Norpoth 2014.

[39] http://www.ilo.org/public/libdoc/ilo/2006/106B09_303_engl.pdf. See Krajewski 2011, pp. 60–61; Rudolph 2005.

[40] http://mneguidelines.oecd.org/text/; see Tully 2001; Krajewski 2011, p. 56; Utz 2011; Huarte Melgar et al. 2011.

standards in employment, protection of the environment, the fight against corruption, consumer protection, competition and taxation, since the 2011 revision, they have contained an explicit paragraph on human rights. Chapter IV states that:

> … Enterprises should, within the framework of internationally recognised human rights, the international human rights obligations of the countries in which they operate as well as relevant domestic laws and regulations:
>
> 1. Respect human rights, which means they should avoid infringing on the human rights of others and should address adverse human rights impacts with which they are involved
> 2. Within the context of their own activities, avoid causing or contributing to adverse human rights impacts and address such impacts when they occur.
> 3. Seek ways to prevent or mitigate adverse human rights impacts that are directly linked to their business operations, products or services by a business relationship, even if they do not contribute to those impacts.
> 4. Have a policy commitment to respect human rights.
> 5. Carry out human rights due diligence as appropriate to their size, the nature and context of operations and the severity of the risks of adverse human rights impacts.
> 6. Provide for or co-operate through legitimate processes in the remediation of adverse human rights impacts where they identify that they have caused or contributed to these impacts.

The commentary on the *Guidelines* which has been published by the OECD highlights the fact that these requirements refer to all of the human rights mentioned in the *International Bill of Rights*, as well as the ILO core labor standards.[41] The *OECD Guidelines* are targeted at all enterprises that operate within or originating from the Signatory States. They are not legally binding, but represent standards to be respected on a voluntary basis, thereby complementing corporate, private initiatives to define and implement *Corporate Social Responsibility* benchmarks. The governments of the Signatory States—currently including 34 OECD Member States and ten other States[42]—are expected to make active efforts in supporting responsible business conduct. In this regard, the so-called *National Contact Points* facilitate the receipt of complaints by NGOs or employer associations on the lack of compliance with the *OECD Guidelines* by individual enterprises. These are merely arbitration bodies and not courts of law. Nevertheless, they have a certain—although, as yet, relatively weak[43]—disciplinary effect as their reports are made accessible to the public.

---

[41] OECD-Guidelines, Commentary on Human Rights, https://mneguidelines.oecd.org/2011HumanRights.pdf, Para 39: "In all cases and irrespective of the country or specific context of enterprises' operations, reference should be made at a minimum to the internationally recognised human rights expressed in the International Bill of Human Rights, consisting of the Universal Declaration of Human Rights and the main instruments through which it has been codified: the International Covenant on Civil and Political Rights and the International Covenant on Economic, Social and Cultural Rights, and to the principles concerning fundamental rights set out in the 1998 International Labour Organisation Declaration on Fundamental Principles and Rights at Work."

[42] http://mneguidelines.oecd.org/ncps/.

[43] See Germanwatch and Misereor 2014, pp. 111–115; Robinson 2014, pp. 71–75.

The attempt on the UN level to fix binding human rights standards in international law for companies has failed for the time being. The Member States represented in the *Commission on Human Rights* have not been able to agree on the *UN Norms of the Responsibility of Transnational Corporations and other Business Enterprises with Regard to Human Rights*[44] which was tabled for debate and adoption in 2003. Disagreements on direct and comprehensive human rights responsibility of business, as postulated in the *UN Norms*, have been too extensive.[45] The multitude of sets of rules that have evolved during the past years under the heading of *Corporate Social Responsibility*, either adopted by individual companies, organized sectorally or originating from multi-stakeholder initiatives (partially with the participation of international organizations or NGOs),[46] are merely to be considered, with regard to their legal status, as expressions of voluntary commitment. Hence, since there is no direct obligation for multinational companies to respect human rights according to the current state of international law, States' extra-territorial obligation to protect remains the only connecting legal factor in this context: States do have the responsibility to abide by human rights norms, not only with regard to those events taking place on their own State territory but also outside it. That means that they are obliged to respect, protect and fulfil human rights on foreign State territory. Of special importance in the context of social human rights is the second stage of extraterritorial State obligations[47]—the obligation to protect—because it is able to bridge a protection gap which has, considering the threats for social rights in the frame of a globalized economy, far-reaching implications. The home States of multinational companies that have taken part in human rights violations abroad must ensure that such violations are restrained and put to an end, and that the concerned companies are brought to justice.

With regard to civil and political rights, this obligation is restricted insofar as the ICCPR contains a jurisdiction clause, according to which "(e)ach State Party to the present Covenant undertakes to respect and to ensure to all individuals within its territory and subject to its jurisdiction the rights recognized in the present Covenant".[48] Thus the *Covenant's* rights are only to be ensured for those persons that are

---

[44] UN Doc. E/CN.4/Sub.2/2003/12/Rev.2, 26.8.2003, http://www1.umn.edu/humanrts/links/norms-Aug2003.html; see Weissbrodt and Kruger 2003; Vagts 2003; Nowrot 2003; Emmerich-Fritsche 2007, pp. 546–547.

[45] For an overview on this discussion see Ssenyonjo 2009, pp. 142–144; De Schutter 2014, pp. 195–217; see also, generally, Köster 2010, pp. 129–130. Although the *UN Norms* have not gone beyond draft status, they have heavily influenced both the academic and political debates on the responsibilities of companies under international law.

[46] The *UN Global Compact* is an important example for such a CSR standard; see https://www.unglobalcompact.org/index.html.

[47] The terminology is inconsistent on this question; also the terms "transnational", "transboundary", "international", "global" or "third state obligations" are used; cf. Gibney 2013.

[48] Article 2(1) ICCPR; for problems related to the interpretation of this clause, cf. Kälin and Künzli 2009, pp. 132–133.

in some way subject to the authority of the State, or to the effective control of a Member State. The intensity of control as required for the acceptance of such an obligation to protect would only be given in case of an occupying regime, long-term security operations or similar instances.[49] However, the ICESCR does not contain a corresponding clause, despite the fact that it was drawn up at the same time as the ICCPR. This should be considered a clear indication that the authors of the ICESCR had assumed an extraterritorial applicability of social rights.[50] Furthermore, it seems quite obvious to define human rights responsibility as reaching beyond a State's own boundaries not only in relation to the respective persons to be protected, but also to focus on non-State actors as potential violators of human rights. This concept, according to which the State also bears human rights responsibility by exercising effective control over such actors who contribute to threatening or even violating human rights is increasingly accepted within the more recent literature on this topic.[51] Yet, regardless of the interpretation of the ICESCR text concerning this issue, the extraterritorial effect is supported not least by the fact that the *erga omnes*-character of certain essential human rights[52] has meanwhile gained recognition in international law. It has been hence rightly noted that those situations where States are concerned about the protection of such essential values are exceptional cases to be treated differently from the "normal case" of extraterritorial jurisdiction that is still disputed.[53]

The *Maastricht Principles on Extraterritorial Obligations of States in the Area of Economic, Social and Cultural Rights*, drawn up in September 2011 by an independent expert commission,[54] put into concrete terms the obligations to protect

---

49 For such an interpretation of the clause see, for example, von Bernstorff 2011, p. 52.

50 Vandenhole 2003, pp. 445–446; Skogly and Gibney 2002, pp. 790–791; De Schutter 2010, p. 163; Papp 2013, p. 119; similarly Skogly 2006, pp. 57–72; for a different view see Kälin and Künzli 2009, pp. 141–142.

51 For an overview of the discussion see von Bernstorff 2011, pp. 55–56; den Heijer and Lawson 2013, pp. 186–190; Papp 2013, pp. 121–122.

52 Bantekas and Oette 2013, pp. 70–71; Goldmann 2014, p. 428. According to van Genugten 1992, p. 19, social rights that have been recognized for a long time are also part of those main human rights that unfold an *erga omnes*-obligation. The *Human Rights Committee* in its *General Comment No. 31* (Nature of the General Legal Obligation on States Parties to the Covenant, U.N. Doc. CCPR/C/21/Rev.1/Add.13, 26.5.2004, http://daccess-dds-ny.un.org/doc/UNDOC/GEN/G04/419/56/PDF/G0441956.pdf?OpenElement, Para 2, even goes further: According to it, all human rights imply an *erga omnes*-effect.

53 De Schutter et al. 2012, p. 1142. : "The erga omnes character of human rights may justify allowing the exercise by states of extraterritorial jurisdiction, even in conditions that might otherwise not be permissible, where such exercise seeks to promote such rights. Similarly, the realization of the MDGs is of interest to all states. Therefore, extraterritorial jurisdiction seeking to promote human rights, or the achievement of the MDGs, is not a case where one state seeks to impose its values on another state, as in other cases of extraterritorial jurisdiction."—In detail on the term of jurisdiction in international human rights protection and in general international law den Heijer and Lawson 2013, pp. 158–182.

54 http://www.etoconsortium.org/en/library/maastricht-principles/; see for an overview Coomans 2012.

that must be respected by States with regard to the behavior of non-governmental actors such as companies outside their sovereign territory. The question of jurisdiction, which is indeed crucial for the extent of potential extraterritorial obligations, is taken up in Principle 9 and is answered in accordance with the more recent interpretation following a broad understanding of the term:

> A State has obligations to respect, protect and fulfil economic, social and cultural rights in any of the following: a) situations over which it exercises authority or effective control, whether or not such control is exercised in accordance with international law; b) situations over which State acts or omissions bring about foreseeable effects on the enjoyment of economic, social and cultural rights, whether within or outside its territory; c) situations in which the State, acting separately or jointly, whether through its executive, legislative or judicial branches, is in a position to exercise decisive influence or to take measures to realize economic, social and cultural rights extraterritorially, in accordance with international law.

Thereupon, a general obligation to regulate is established in Principle 24:

> All States must take necessary measures to ensure that non-State actors which they are in a position to regulate, as set out in Principle 25, such as private individuals and organizations, and transnational corporations and other business enterprises, do not nullify or impair the enjoyment of economic, social and cultural rights. These include administrative, legislative, investigative, adjudicatory and other measures. All other States have a duty to refrain from nullifying or impairing the discharge of this obligation to protect.

Principle 25 further elaborates which companies are covered by this obligation to regulate[55]:

> States must adopt and enforce measures to protect economic, social and cultural rights through legal and other means, including diplomatic means, in each of the following circumstances: a) – b) … c) as regards business enterprises, where the corporation, or its parent or controlling company, has its centre of activity, is registered or domiciled, or has its main place of business or substantial business activities, in the State concerned; d) where there is a reasonable link between the State concerned and the conduct it seeks to regulate, including where relevant aspects of a non-State actor's activities are carried out in that State's territory; e) …[56]

[55] The even stricter standard of Principle 12 applies to companies that are partly owned or controlled by the state: "State responsibility extends to: (a) acts and omissions of non-State actors acting on the instructions or under the direction or control of the State; and (b) acts and omissions of persons or entities which are not organs of the State, such as corporations and other business enterprises, where they are empowered by the State to exercise elements of governmental authority, provided those persons or entities are acting in that capacity in the particular instance."

[56] In their comment on the *Maastricht Principles* De Schutter et al. 2012, p. 1141, give examples where a relation between a State and a transnationally operating company can be established via Princ. 25(d): "Examples of instances where a state should take action to protect rights under Principle 25(d) … include situations where a non-state actor accused of human rights abuse in another country has assets that can be seized in order to implement the judgment of a competent court where there may be relevant evidence or witnesses, where relevant officials accused of criminal liability may be present, or where the non-state actor may have carried out part of the operations that resulted in the abuse."

Additionally, the *Maastricht Principles* provide a regulation for those cases where a State does not have the possibility to regulate, due to legal or factual reasons, but where it can influence in other ways the activities of companies operating abroad:

> States that are in a position to influence the conduct of non-State actors even if they are not in a position to regulate such conduct, such as through their public procurement system or international diplomacy, should exercise such influence, in accordance with the Charter of the United Nations and general international law, in order to protect economic, social and cultural rights.[57]

The *Maastricht Principles* were not adopted by a conference of States and thus do not possess direct legally binding status. Nevertheless, they reflect the progressing current opinion in international law on this issue.[58] Recently, in September 2013, several UN experts on human rights highlighted the importance of this document for the development of international protection of human rights.[59] Moreover, it should certainly not be overlooked that previously and on several occasions, the CESCR also mentioned the different dimensions of extraterritorial obligations of States in its *General Comments*, and put particular emphasis on the second dimension, the international obligation to protect. Accordingly, the following is stated in *General Comment No. 15*:

> Steps should be taken by States parties to prevent their own citizens and companies from violating the right to water of individuals and communities in other countries …[60]

---

[57] Principle 26 *Maastricht Principles*. See in this context Germanwatch and Misereor 2014, pp. 35–69 (This report offers—by using the example of the Federal Republic of Germany—an informative overview of instruments available for states to influence activities of companies outside their own state territory in order to prevent human rights violations.), and, generally, also Ryngart 2013, pp. 204–207.

[58] See, for example, Künnemann 2004, pp. 219–220; Sepúlveda Carmona 2009, p. 91.

[59] Human rights beyond borders: UN experts call on world governments to be guided by the Maastricht Principles, http://www.ohchr.org/EN/NewsEvents/Pages/DisplayNews.aspx?NewsID=13792&LangID=E.: "28 September 2011 was a significant moment in the development of international human rights law … The Maastricht Principles filled a critical gap in the international legal framework, allowing human rights to effectively respond to the negative impacts of globalisation that cannot be regulated by one State alone." Cf. also the *Final draft of the guiding principles on extreme poverty and human rights*, submitted by the Special Rapporteur on extreme poverty and human rights, Magdalena Sepúlveda Carmona, UN Doc. A/HRC/21/39, 18.7.2012, http://daccess-dds-ny.un.org/doc/UNDOC/GEN/G12/154/60/PDF/G1215460.pdf?OpenElement, Paras 92, 93.

[60] CESCR 2003, Para 33. A similar wording can be found in the *Statement of the CESCR on the Obligations of States Parties Regarding the Corporate Sector and Economic, Social and Cultural Rights*, U.N. Doc. E/C.12/2011/1, 20.5.2011, Para 5: "States Parties should also take steps to prevent human rights contraventions abroad by corporations which have their main seat under their jurisdiction, without infringing the sovereignty or diminishing the obligations of the host States under the Covenant."

One may consider this formulation as a mere request to States to adapt their legal policy; however, the demand to comply with extraterritorial obligations to protect was made considerably more explicit some years later in *General Comment No. 19*:

> To comply with their international obligations in relation to the right to social security, States parties have to respect the enjoyment of the right by refraining from actions that interfere, directly or indirectly, with the enjoyment of the right to social security in other countries.[61] … States parties should extraterritorially protect the right to social security by preventing their own citizens and national entities from violating this right in other countries. …[62]

The concept of obligations to protect also represents the core of the *UN Guiding Principles on Business and Human Rights*,[63] adopted unanimously in 2011 by the *Human Rights Council*, thereby replacing the *UN Norms* which had previously failed, due to the resistance of several States and trade associations, in particular.[64] While there is no immediate legal obligation for companies, according to the *UN Guiding Principles*, but only a corporate responsibility to respect human rights,[65] the States are requested to protect their populations from interference by companies in human rights by implementing regulatory measures and appropriate complaint and sanction mechanisms.[66] However, the *UN Guiding Principles* remain vague on the issue of extraterritorial obligations:

> States should set out clearly the expectation that all business enterprises domiciled in their territory and/or jurisdiction respect human rights throughout their operations.[67]

---

[61] CESCR 2008, Para 53.

[62] CESCR 2008, Para 54. The UN Special Representative John Ruggie, however, assumes that this is merely a recommendation, see *Report of the Special Representative of the Secretary-General on the issue of human rights and transnational corporations and other business enterprises* ("Business and human rights: Towards operationalizing the 'protect, respect and remedy' framework"), UN-Doc. A/HRC/11/13, 22.04.2009, http://www2.ohchr.org/english/bodies/hrcouncil/docs/11session/A.HRC.11.13.pdf, Para 15.

[63] *Guiding Principles on Business and Human Rights: Implementing the United Nations "Protect, Respect and Remedy" Framework*, UN Doc. A/HRC/17/31, 21.3.2011, http://www.ohchr.org/Documents/Issues/Business/A-HRC-17-31_AEV.pdf; see for a detailed discussion of the *UN Guiding Principles* Jägers 2011; Mares 2012; Windfuhr 2012, pp. 106–113; von Bernstorff 2012b; de la Vega et al. 2011; Massoud 2013; Tietje 2013, pp. 277–280; Germanwatch and Misereor 2014, pp. 29–32.

[64] Cf. International Organisation of Employers/International Chamber of Commerce, Joint views of the IOE and ICC on the draft "Norms on the responsibilities of transnational corporations and other business enterprises with regard to human rights", March 2004, http://198.170.85.29/IOE-ICC-views-UN-norms-March-2004.doc.

[65] Companies are expected to avoid human rights violations and infringements of core labor rights norms and to adapt their corporate policy accordingly; applicable tools are, inter alia, public policy commitments and the realization of human rights due diligence procedures; see in detail *UN Guiding Principles,* Paras 11–24.

[66] Paras 1–10 *UN Guiding Principles.*

[67] Para 2 *UN Guiding Principles.*

The commentary on this provision points out that there might be good reasons for governments to encourage companies also to respect human rights in their operations abroad, but there is currently no express legal obligation.[68]

Despite this, a more recent UN document, the *Voluntary Guidelines on the Responsible Governance of Tenure of Land, Fisheries and Forests in the Context of National Food Security*, shows a considerable shift of emphasis towards international recognition of an extraterritorial obligation to protect. The *Guidelines* were developed by the FAO, together with the participation of civil society and the private industry, and were adopted unanimously in May 2012 by the *Committee on World Food Security*.[69] They include standards on political and legal management of agricultural investments, which have been made recently in developing countries on a large scale, but have often been subject to heavy criticism, due to their negative impact on land use by local small farmers (so-called "land grabbing"[70]). Just as in the *UN Guiding Principles*, the *FAO Guidelines* address private investors as well as States: The companies are requested to respect human rights and legitimate land use rights, and to conduct, in particular, the necessary due diligence investigations[71]; direct international legal obligations are not imposed. In this respect, the *FAO Guidelines* follow the pattern of the *UN Guiding Principles*. For States, however, a stricter standard applies; they are obliged to implement land use policies compatible with human rights via appropriate regulatory measures. Their extraterritorial obligations are addressed twice within the document:

> … Where transnational corporations are involved, their home States have roles to play in assisting both those corporations and host States to ensure that businesses are not involved in abuse of human rights and legitimate tenure rights. States should take additional steps to protect against abuses of human rights and legitimate tenure rights by business enterprises that are owned or controlled by the State, or that receive substantial support and service from State agencies.[72] … When States invest or promote investments abroad, they should ensure that their conduct is consistent with the protection of legitimate tenure rights, the promotion of food security and their existing obligations under national and international law, and with due regard to voluntary commitments under applicable regional and international instruments.[73]

Hence, the *FAO Guidelines* go discernibly beyond the requirements of the *UN Guiding Principles* on this matter. The fact that the UN, for the first time, has explicitly recognized the existence of legal obligations of States with regard to entrepreneurial activities abroad[74] represents undoubtedly remarkable progress in the development of the international protection of human rights. At the same time,

---

[68] Ibid.

[69] http://www.fao.org/fileadmin/user_upload/nr/land_tenure/pdf/VG_en_Final_March_2012.pdf; see von Bernstorff 2012a; Seufert 2014.

[70] See infra Sect. 4.1.

[71] Para 3.2 *FAO Guidelines*.

[72] Ibid.

[73] Para 12.5 *FAO Guidelines*.

[74] von Bernstorff 2012a, pp. 40–41.

they support the thesis presented here: The concept of extraterritorial obligations to protect, as it has been drawn up in the 2011 *Maastricht Principles* for the human rights guaranteed in the IESCR, already complies with the current state of international law.

3.3 Extraterritorial Obligations to Fulfil Social Rights: Is There a Legal Duty to Provide Development Assistance?

Overcoming global poverty is a task concerning both the South and the North. Nowadays, no one would seriously deny this fact—as countless resolutions of the *UN General Assembly* and outcome documents of international conferences have repeatedly confirmed. It is, however, less known that this shared political responsibility also has a legal dimension. The legal responsibility arises, on the one hand, generally from the *UN Charter* which requires "universal respect for, and observance of, human rights and fundamental freedoms for all"[75] and obliges the Member States "to take joint and separate action in co-operation with the Organization", inter alia to achieve this very aim of global protection of human rights.[76] With regard to the realization of social rights in particular, the ICESCR contains an additional unambiguous statement: Article 2(1) obliges the States Parties explicitly to aim individually and "through international assistance and cooperation, especially economic and technical" at the realization of rights established by the Covenant. This stipulation is also supported procedurally: According to Article 14 OP, the Committee is obliged to contact the competent specialized agencies and programs of the UN after completion of a procedure included in the OP (inter alia individual complaints mechanism and inquiry procedure, see supra Sect. 1.1) in order to enable them to take appropriate measures to support the concerned countries.

One of the three dimensions of the so-called extraterritorial obligations of States —the extraterritorial obligation to fulfil—is expressed in the duty to provide international assistance under the ICESCR. According to this specification of the principle of solidarity in international law[77] the States Parties to the Covenant shall also actively engage in the implementation of their treaty obligations outside their territories. The *Maastricht Principles*[78] put in more concrete terms the extraterritorial obligation to fulfil. Firstly, it is highlighted that the obligations to fulfil are by no means limited to official development assistance (ODA), as the spectrum of topics covered by international obligations to cooperate manifests right at the beginning of the relevant chapter:

---

[75] Article 55 lit. c UN.

[76] Article 56 UN.

[77] Cf. Dann 2010.

[78] See supra Sect. 2.3.

> States must take deliberate, concrete and targeted steps, separately, and jointly through international cooperation, to create an international enabling environment conducive to the universal fulfilment of economic, social and cultural rights, including in matters relating to bilateral and multilateral trade, investment, taxation, finance, environmental protection, and development cooperation. The compliance with this obligation is to be achieved through, inter alia: (a) elaboration, interpretation, application and regular review of multilateral and bilateral agreements as well as international standards; (b) measures and policies by each State in respect of its foreign relations, including actions within international organizations, and its domestic measures and policies that can contribute to the fulfilment of economic, social and cultural rights extraterritorially.[79]

Nevertheless, development cooperation is a crucial component of the obligation to fulfil; hence the authors of the *Maastricht Principles* dedicate a separate paragraph to it:

> As part of the broader obligation of international cooperation, States, acting separately and jointly, that are in a position to do so, must provide international assistance to contribute to the fulfilment of economic, social and cultural rights in other States, …[80]

By means of this clause, the authors of the *Maastricht Principles* make clear that there exists a general obligation of the industrialized States to provide official development assistance to poorer members of the international community.[81] Such a concrete entitlement to assistance is, however, disputed in the international law literature: Some authors assume that the genesis of the ICESCR is an argument against such an obligation.[82] Others are of the opinion that a legal obligation to assistance does indeed exist, but only in exceptional circumstances, such as famines or in other instances of humanitarian crisis.[83] The wording of Article 2(1) ICESCR and the lack of a jurisdiction clause as contained in the ICCPR,[84] however, suggest

---

79 Principle 29 *Maastricht Principles*; cf. also Salomon 2013, pp. 262–263.

80 Principle 33 *Maastricht Principles.*

81 In their commentary on the *Maastricht Principles*, De Schutter et al. 2012, p. 1157, rightly point out that this provision is to be understood widely, i.e. covering also other supporting benefits in addition to ODA transfers: "International assistance may, and depending on the circumstances must, comprise other measures, including provision of information to people in other countries, or cooperation with their state, for example, to trace stolen public funds or to cooperate in the adoption of measures to prevent human trafficking".

82 See, for example, Alston and Quinn 1987, pp. 186–192.

83 Sepúlveda 2006, p. 288; Gondek 2009, p. 363; Coomans 2011, p. 27; Dann 2012, pp. 253–254.

84 See supra Sect. 3.2 . See in this context also den Heijer and Lawson 2013, p. 184, who point out that the general duties of international cooperation which are laid down in the ICESCR "are obviously (and deliberately) formulated in broad and general terms, and their very nature would appear to oppose an interpretation that they should be made dependent upon specific conduct or involvements of a State—other than, perhaps, the resources the State has at its disposal. We would uphold the proposition that those duties should accordingly not be made on the existence of a specific 'jurisdictional link' between the State and a particular individual or group of individuals present in a foreign territory. … The omission of a general jurisdiction clause in the ICESCR underscores that the duty of international cooperation and assistance does not necessarily depend upon a prior 'jurisdictional link'."

the favoring of the approach laid down in the *Maastricht Principles*.[85] Also, the CESCR has taken the same position:

> (I)n accordance with Articles 55 and 56 of the Charter of the United Nations, with well-established principles of international law, and with the provisions of the Covenant itself, international cooperation for development and thus for the realization of economic, social and cultural rights is an obligation of all States. It is particularly incumbent upon those States which are in a position to assist others in this regard.[86]

The fact that—notwithstanding this obligation of wealthier States to supply development aid—the primary responsibility for the implementation of social rights remains with those States where the concerned people are situated, is made clear even twice in the *Maastricht Principles*:

> A State has the obligation to fulfil economic, social and cultural rights in its territory to the maximum of its ability. …[87] A State has the obligation to seek international assistance and cooperation on mutually agreed terms when that State is unable, despite its best efforts, to guarantee economic, social and cultural rights within its territory. That State has an obligation to ensure that assistance provided is used towards the realization of economic, social and cultural rights.[88]

The extraterritorial obligation of industrialized countries to support poorer States in their efforts to implement duties under the ICESCR thus involves, respectively, solely a complementary (or subsidiary) responsibility,[89] whose actual relevance is, nevertheless, not to be underestimated considering the extent of global poverty.[90]

The proposal made in the *Maastricht Principles* for a regulatory framework for extraterritorial obligations of States may certainly not solve all problems: In particular, the issue of defining the exact allocation and the concrete extent of the obligations to assist is persistent.[91] While this is less problematic for correlations of

---

[85] For a similar opinion see Hennessy 2002, pp. 86–88; Skogly 2006, p. 193; Ssenyonjo 2009, pp. 69–81; Ziegler et al. 2011, p. 83; cf. furthermore Craven 1995, p. 149; very clearly also Pogge 2005, p. 741: "Given that the present global institutional order is foreseeably associated with such massive incidence of avoidable severe poverty, its (uncompensated) imposition manifests an ongoing human rights violation—arguably the largest such violation ever committed in human history. … The continuing imposition of this global order, essentially unmodified, constitutes a massive violation of the human right to basic necessities—a violation for which the governments and electorates of the more powerful countries bear primary responsibility."; for a more skeptical view see Dann 2012, p. 208 (with further references).

[86] Cf. CESCR 1990, Para 14; CESCR 2000, Para 39; CESCR 2003, Para 38; CESCR 2001, Para 17.

[87] Principle 31 *Maastricht Principles*.

[88] Principle 34 *Maastricht Principles*.

[89] Vandenhole and Benedek 2013, p. 335; Salomon 2013, p. 278.

[90] Salomon 2013, p. 279.

[91] For an analysis of causation problems in this context see Skogly 2013; Salomon 2013; cf. also Dann 2012, pp. 239–242, who makes convincing arguments in favor of an application of the rules on complicity to substantiate the development aid donor's responsibility for human rights violations in the recipient State.

For a slightly different approach see also Coomans 2011, p. 27.

responsibility with a distinct bilateral reference, global and multipolar development issues make it difficult to attribute exact quantifiable obligations to certain States in relation to other actors. The provisions of the *Maastricht Principles* remain—inevitably—rather vague, as they state that

> (e)ach State must separately and, where necessary, jointly contribute to the fulfilment of economic, social and cultural rights ...[92]

Even though proposals for how to achieve a more precise determination of legally required assistance in the context of development cooperation have already been developed in the literature,[93] one must proceed from the assumption that most donor States—at least beyond bilateral contractual commitments—would rather not accept a general legal obligation for the contribution of a (more or less) clearly defined amount of development aid in the near future.[94] Even the target of 0.7 %, which has served for many decades as a point of reference for the duties of donor States, and which has also been repeatedly demanded by the CESCR,[95] has been recognized only politically, but not been incorporated yet into a binding international treaty.[96] The procedural obligations to coordinate assistance, as stipulated in Para 30 of the *Maastricht Principles*, are considered an attempt to handle allocation and quantification issues in development cooperation, based on the principle of *common but differentiated responsibilities among States*.[97] However, in the case

---

[92] Principle 31, 2 *Maastricht Principles*. The CESCR has pointed out that the extent of legally required international assistance follows, according to the extent of territorial obligations, maximum return; see CESCR 1990, Para 3: "The Committee notes that the phrase 'to the maximum of its available resources' was intended by the drafters of the Covenant to refer to both the resources existing within a State and those available from the international community through international cooperation and assistance." Salomon (2007, p. 101) has rightly criticized that "the very approach enshrined in the Covenant presents a perverse (albeit predictable) logic; it is concerned what a state can afford to do by its own estimation rather than what needs to be done to secure the minimum essential levels of economic, social and cultural rights globally."; in this context, cf. also Donati and Vidar 2008, p. 65.

[93] Khalfan 2013, pp. 324–328; Vandenhole and Benedek 2013, pp. 340–350.

[94] In the past, individual industrialized countries have repeatedly made clear that they consider themselves morally committed to development cooperation, but do not recognize corresponding legal obligations; cf. the *Report of the Open-ended Working Group to Consider Options regarding the Elaboration of an Optional Protocol to the International Covenant on Economic, Social and Cultural Rights on its second session*, UN Doc. E/CN.4/2005/52, 10.2.2005, Para 76; see also Gondek 2009, pp. 328–333.

[95] See Ssenyonjo 2009, p. 79 (with references in Fn. 202–206). For the discussion on the calculation of financial means which are needed to reach the MDGs see, for example, Sachs 2005, pp. 353–374.

[96] The target of 0,7 % of GNP to be allocated to development cooperation by each State has been formulated for the first time by the *UN General Assembly* in 1970 (UN Doc. A/RES/25/2626 [XXV], 24.10.1970, Para 43) and since then has been affirmed several times; cf. for more details Vandenhole and Benedek 2013, p. 347.

[97] De Schutter et al. 2012, pp. 1149–1150. See also generally on the procedural approach in the law of development cooperation Salomon 2007, p. 102: "International cooperation favours obligations of conduct: process over outcome, conduct over result, assurances of best effort over

that development aid is de facto provided, certain priority criteria apply which can be derived directly from the ICESCR. Despite the margin of discretion that is left to States with regard to the optimal allocation of resources available to them, they are requested to respect certain criteria due to their human rights obligations:

> In fulfiling economic, social and cultural rights extraterritorially, States must: (a) prioritize the realization of the rights of disadvantaged, marginalized and vulnerable groups; (b) prioritize core obligations to realize minimum essential levels of economic, social and cultural rights, and move as expeditiously and effectively as possible towards the full realization of economic, social and cultural rights. ...[98]

Furthermore, where a State opts for a long-term reduction of development assistance without giving comprehensible justification for it, an act of violation against international law can be assumed.[99]

Even though today the *Maastricht Principles*—as well as the CESCR *General Comments*—are merely designated as international *soft law* , they are nevertheless of crucial importance to international cooperation between industrialized and developing countries: The concept of extraterritorial obligations of States provides an international law framework that might allow the structuring of relations of responsibility between the North and the South—as long as they concern issues on human development—in a balanced and generally acceptable way. As a whole, the *Maastricht Principles* therefore present an important complement to other international standards—such as the MDGs, the *Monterrey Consensus*,[100] the documents on Aid Effectiveness concluded at the *High Level Forums* in Paris, Accra and Busan[101] and the *ILO Social Protection Floor* Initiative[102]—which have by now gained global recognition as either procedural or textual blueprints for development cooperation. They are of special importance to the *Post 2015-Development Agenda*, as they underline the fact that, besides the general obligation to international cooperation according to the *UN Charter*, an explicit international legal obligation of all IESCR Contracting States exists to contribute to global poverty alleviation, not least by intensifying their commitment in the field of development aid.

(Footnote 97 continued)
guarantees of success. ... Political commitments towards international cooperation have been recently articulated as 'global partnerships for development', provided for in the 8th Millennium Development Goal."

98 Principle 32 *Maastricht Principles*; see also Kämpf and Winkler 2012, pp. 78–80.

99 Cf. Craven 1995, p. 150.

100 *Monterrey Consensus on Financing for Development*, UN Doc. A/AC.257/32, 22.3.2002, http://www.un.org/esa/ffd/monterrey/MonterreyConsensus.pdf; *Doha Declaration on Financing for Development: Outcome document of the Follow-up International Conference on Financing for Development to Review the Implementation of the Monterrey Consensus*, annexed to GA res. 63/239, UN Doc. A/RES/63/239, 2.12.2008, http://www.un.org/esa/ffd/doha/documents/Doha_Declaration_FFD.pdf.

101 http://www.oecd.org/dac/effectiveness/34428351.pdf; http://www.oecd.org/dac/effectiveness/49650173.pdf.

102 See infra Sect. 5.2.

3.4 Social Rights Obligations of the International Financial Institutions and the World Trade Organization

Nowadays, among the most important stakeholders in development cooperation are international organizations operating worldwide, such as the *World Bank* and the numerous development bodies of the UN. It is disputed among experts on international law whether these organizations are legally bound to respect human rights. On the one hand, they are not contracting parties of human rights treaties and have therefore no direct obligation under these treaties. On the other hand, their existence is based on international agreements whose contracting parties are—at least predominantly—also Signatory States of the main human rights conventions. It is, therefore, reasonable to hold the argument that international organizations are, at least, indirectly bound to respect human rights. This is of practical relevance, for example, to major infrastructure projects that are carried out in developing and emerging countries with financial means provided by the *World Bank.*[103] Constructions of dams and large-scale irrigation projects have often been related to displacement of the local population. In these cases, aggrieved people were faced with some serious impairment of their rights to property, but also of their rights to adequate housing, food and health.[104] Furthermore, the *World Bank*, but also the IMF, were accused of supporting, inter alia, dictatorial and repressive regimes with their lending policies, and thereby of contributing to their human rights violations.[105] Despite the protest of the *UN General Assembly*, the former South African apartheid regime was granted financial aid by the international financial institutions,[106] but also more recently other governments which are not known at all for an immaculate human rights track record have managed to obtain credit. Moreover, the structural adjustment programs of the *World Bank* and the IMF have been subject to heavy criticism. In the 1980s, they had led to serious socio-political problems and, as such, to infringements of social human rights, particularly in many poorer developing countries, due to the radical economic reforms which debtors were required to carry out (consolidation of the national budget by cutbacks in expenditure in the public sector and by privatization).[107]

Besides the financial organizations, the WTO is to be mentioned in this context. Though it is not a classical development organization,[108] it is committed to

---

[103] For a discussion of the human rights obligations of the *World Bank* and other international financial institutions see Skogly 2001; Darrow 2003, van Genugten et al. 2003; Ghazi 2005; Fujita 2013.

[104] See Janik 2012, pp. 120–121, 128–131 with further references.

[105] A prominent critic of IMF is Jean Ziegler, who considers this organization—alongside with WTO—to the "most crucial enemies of economic, social and cultural human rights, especially of the right to food" (2011, p. 158; own translation).

[106] Cf. Darrow 2003, pp. 150–152.

[107] Darrow 2003, pp. 104–105; Goldmann 2014, pp. 428–429; Janik 2012, pp. 123–128.

[108] On this issue see also Krajewski 2014, pp. 273–274; Qureshi 2009.

development policy objectives according to the preamble of the agreement under which it was established, and has emphasized important features in this policy field, not least with the *Doha Development Agenda*.[109] The WTO has frequently been criticized in the past for not attaching enough importance to respect for social human rights in its decisions.[110] One important example is the practice of industrialized nations, tolerated for a long time by international trade law, of supporting their farmers via export subsidies to such a degree that agricultural production in developing countries was massively damaged—at least in certain sectors—and that consequently food security for the population considerably deteriorated.[111] As yet, the issue of subsidies leading to distortions of competition on the international agricultural markets has not been adequately solved, even though the first successful steps have been taken on the way to fairer international trade conditions.[112] Another example is the right to health, which conflicts with WTO trade regulations, because patent protection guaranteed by TRIPS has a negative impact on the production of generic drugs which are especially needed in developing countries. Due to exemption regulations from TRIPS, some improvements have also been made during the last years in this field[113]; however, it is still difficult for many poorer countries to overcome the high bureaucratic obstacles which are prescribed

[109] *Ministerial Declaration* WT/MIN(01)/DEC/1, 20.11.2001, http://www.wto.org/english/thewto_e/minist_e/min01_e/mindecl_e.htm. Krajewski (2014, pp. 260–261), however, attributes a primarily "rhetoric relevance" to the term "development" in the *Doha Round* (with reference to Jawara and Kwa 2003, p. 266; Qureshi 2009, p. 173); critically also Feyder 2010, p. 181; on the current state of the negotiations see Elsig and Dupont 2012; Erixon 2014; cf. also the 11th revised draft report of the ILA-International Trade Law Committee (ITLC), http://www.ila-hq.org/en/committees/index.cfm/cid/24, Paras 5–8.

[110] This has been emphasized, for example, in the Preliminary report "Globalization and its impact on the full enjoyment of human rights", submitted to the UN Human Rights Commission, Doc. E/CN.4/Sub.2/2000/13, 15.6.2000, http://daccess-dds-ny.un.org/doc/UNDOC/GEN/G00/140/14/PDF/G0014014.pdf?OpenElement, Para 15: "(F)or certain sectors of humanity—particularly the developing countries of the South—the WTO is a veritable nightmare"; for a similar appreciation cf. Ziegler 2011, pp. 167–177. On the relevance of human rights for world trade law see, generally, Cottier et al. 2005; Hilf and Hörmann 2005; Harrison 2007; Hilpold 2007; Joseph et al. 2009; Joseph 2011; Brown 2012; Hestermeyer 2014; Drache and Jacobs 2014.

[111] Cf. the reports by the Special Rapporteurs on the right to food, Jean Ziegler, UN Doc. E/CN.4/2002/58, 10.1.2002, http://www.righttofood.org/wp-content/uploads/2012/09/ECN.4200258.pdf, Paras 111–114; and Olivier De Schutter, UN Doc. A/HRC/10/5/Add.2, 4.2.2009, http://daccess-dds-ny.un.org/doc/UNDOC/GEN/G09/106/39/PDF/G0910639.pdf?OpenElement, Paras 11–13, 16. For further references on this subject see infra Sect. 4.1.1.

[112] On the outcome of the 9th WTO-Ministerial Conference in Bali 2013 see https://www.wto.org/english/thewto_e/minist_e/mc9_e/brief_agneg_e.htm#exportsubsidies; see also Felbermayr et al. 2014; Schmucker 2014.

[113] A concise introduction to this topic and a compilation of new international legal developments can be found at http://www.wto.org/english/tratop_e/trips_e/pharmpatent_e.htm; see, generally, on the TRIPS-pharmaceuticals debate WHO 2006; cf. also Correa 2003; Cullet 2003; Stoll 2005; Hestermeyer 2007; Dreyfuss 2010; Yamane 2011, pp. 261–344; Xiong 2012.

for an exemption from the respective patent protection regulations.[114] Ultimately, as a sub-sector of the WTO regulatory framework, which can be potentially problematic for social rights, the GATS needs to be addressed here: Due to the tendency of some States to privatize, at least partially, the water and health supply for example, conflicts with relevant social rights might arise.[115]

From an international law perspective, international organizations are not typical addressees of human rights obligations. International human rights treaties are aimed at States. Therefore, direct obligations for the WTO, the development banks or the IMF arising out of these treaties can be ruled out.[116] However, since some of these international organizations, such as IBRD and IDA, for example, are specialized agencies of the UN, at least indirect human rights obligations apply nonetheless. This is because the respective provisions in Articles 55c and 56 UN,[117] obliging UN Member States to promote human rights, can be applicable to specialized agencies in accordance with Article 59 UN.[118] Furthermore, directly relevant human rights obligations might arise from the mandate and other organizational rules of these organizations. However, the foundation documents are not particularly abundant in this regard: Looking closely at the mandate of the *World Bank*, for example, its task is "(t)o assist in the reconstruction and development of territories of members by facilitating the investment of capital for productive purposes"[119]; however, a search for references to the relevance of human rights on projects financed by IBRD in the *Articles of Agreement* will be in vain.[120] Instead, some of its provisions, containing more specific details of its mandate, have lately even been interpreted as an indication that the *World Bank* must not deal with human rights issues.[121] It is stated in its Article III Section 5 lit.(b):

---

[114] Hilf and Hörmann 2005, p. 429; see also Howse and Teitel 2009, pp. 62–64; Joseph 2011, pp. 226–230.

[115] See Report of the High Commissioner, Economic Social and Cultural Rights, Liberalization of Trade in Services and Human Rights, UN-Dok. E/CN.4/Sub.2/2002/9, 25.6.2002; furthermore Türk and Krajewski 2004; Hilf and Hörmann 2005, pp. 439–441; McBeth 2010, 150–158; Shawkat et al. 2011, and infra Sect. 4.1.2.

[116] On the question whether financial institutions are guilty of assisting human rights violations by the debtor State due to their more or less „dictated" conditions of loan granting, cf. Janik 2012, pp. 118–119 (with further references). Sometimes it is also argued that a certain core list of human rights has developed an *erga omnes*-effect in the meanwhile, so that they have to be considered in all legal relationships and that they are therewith also binding for international financial institutions; see supra Sect. 3.2 and Buergenthal and Thürer 2009, p. 162.

[117] See supra Sect. 2.3.

[118] See in detail Dann, pp. 246–247; sometimes an (indirect) human rights obligation of the *World Bank* and IMF arising out of Article 103 UN is assumed; see, for example, Ssenyonjo 2009, pp. 131–132.

[119] Article I *IBRD Articles of Agreement*, http://siteresources.worldbank.org/BODINT/Resources/278027-1215526322295/IBRDArticlesOfAgreement_English.pdf; see also Roos 2007, p. 356.

[120] The same applies for other international financial institutions, see Buergenthal and Thürer 2009, p. 157.

[121] Shihata 1995, p. 574.

> The Bank shall make arrangements to ensure that the proceeds of any loan are used only for the purposes for which the loan was granted, with due attention to considerations of economy and efficiency and without regard to political or other non-economic influences or considerations.

This limitation of tasks of the Bank is expressed even more clearly in Article X of the *Articles of Agreement*:

> The Bank and its officers shall not interfere in the political affairs of any member; nor shall they be influenced in their decisions by the political character of the member or members concerned. Only economic considerations shall be relevant to their decisions, …[122]

Today, there is broad consensus that these clauses—which originate from a time before the adoption of the UDHR—at least do not hinder the *World Bank* from taking into consideration human rights standards in policy implementation.[123] Nevertheless an explicit—and legally relevant—commitment to human rights is still lacking in the organizational rules of the Bank. The safeguard policies developed in the 1990s, establishing environmental and social impacts assessments for *World Bank* projects, cover some provisions on the consideration of participation rights for the population group affected by the projects.[124] A comprehensive human rights safeguard policy has not yet been developed, however.[125] Statements included in the document "Development and Human Rights: The Role of the World Bank", published in 1998, in which the *World Bank* tries to set forth the compatibility of its lending policy with human rights,[126] can also not be used to justify a

---

[122] The *IMF Articles of Agreement* (http://www.imf.org/External/Pubs/FT/AA/) do not contain such a ban on political activity, however the IMF is even more reluctant than the IBRD to recognize the human rights relevance of its operation; see Janik 2012, p. 297.

[123] Darrow 2003, p. 192, Oberleitner 2007, pp. 131–132; Janik 2012, pp. 359–387; see also Herdegen 2014, § 192, Para 130.

[124] Janik 2012, pp. 274–279.

[125] Buergenthal and Thürer 2009, p. 160; Ssenyonjo 2009, p. 133. In the draft of the Bank's new *Environmental and Social Framework* ("Setting Standards for Sustainable Development"; see http://consultations.worldbank.org/Data/hub/files/consultation-template/review-and-update-world-bank-safeguard-policies/en/materials/first_draft_framework_july_30_2014.pdf) only few indications on a changed perspective on human rights can be found (e.g. in p. 5 Para 3 "… the Bank's operations are supportive of human rights and will encourage respect for them in a manner consistent with the Bank's Articles of Agreement."); on the review of the *World Bank Safeguard Policies* see also http://web.worldbank.org/WBSITE/EXTERNAL/PROJECTS/EXTPOLICIES/EXTSAFEPOL/0,,contentMDK:23277451~pagePK:64168445~piPK:64168309~theSitePK:584435,00.html; furthermore von Bernstorff and Dann 2013; Scheper 2013.

[126] World Bank 1998, p. 3: "The Bank contributes directly to the fulfillment of many rights articulated in the Universal Declaration. Through its support of primary education, health care and nutrition, sanitation, housing, and the environment, the Bank has helped hundreds of millions of people attain crucial economic and social rights. In other areas, the Bank's contributions are necessarily less direct, but perhaps equally significant. By helping to fight corruption, improve transparency and accountability in governance, strengthen judicial systems, and modernize financial sectors, the Bank contributes to building environments in which people are better able to pursue a broader range of human rights." and p. 30: "For the World Bank, protecting and advancing human rights means helping the world's poorest people escape poverty."

legal (self-)obligation. Even though the *World Bank* has, so far, not explicitly accepted a legal obligation to respect human rights,[127] a clear tendency to greater attention towards human rights can be observed recently in its growing efforts during planning and implementation of *World Bank*-funded development projects, to focus more intensively on the fulfilment of good governance-standards in the respective countries,[128] and to cushion negative socio-political effects of its lending policy with social safety nets.[129] Furthermore, the *World Bank*'s unambiguous commitment to directing its policy primarily towards the objective of poverty reduction is to be acknowledged as an important, albeit only indirect, contribution to the realization of social human rights.[130]

A slightly different situation is prevailing in international trade law: Human rights are neither mentioned in the *Agreement Establishing the WTO*,[131] nor in the individual agreements that are part of the overall regulatory framework of the organization.[132] A mere indirect reference to human rights can be found in the *Doha Development Agenda*. Para 6 of the *Ministerial Declaration* highlights that

---

[127] In the "Legal Opinion on Human Rights and the Work of the World Bank" of 27.1.2006, authored by the *World Bank* General Counsel Roberto Danino (see for excerpts of the text McBeth et al. 2011, pp. 644–645), a direct legal obligation of the Bank to comply with human rights has not been recognized; however the document makes clear that the Bank is aware of the importance of human rights for its work: "(T)he Bank has a significant role in helping member countries in the substantive realization of their human rights obligations in areas that fall within the remit of its mandate and where development activities and human rights are deeply interrelated. This is particularly important in cases where countries request such an assistance, or where they frame questions or strategies related to poverty reduction or development in human rights terms. It is therefore legitimate for the Bank to take human rights into consideration as part of its economic decision-making process." See also World Bank, A Proposal for a Comprehensive Development Framework (A Discussion Draft), 1999, http://web.worldbank.org/WBSITE/EXTERNAL/EXTABOUTUS/EXTWEBARCHIVES/0,,MDK:22201409~menuPK:64654237~pagePK:64660187~piPK:64660385~theSitePK:2564958,00.html, Part 1 A. 2.: "Without the protection of human and property rights, and a comprehensive framework of laws, no equitable development is possible. A government must ensure that it has an effective system of property, contract, labor, bankruptcy, commercial codes, personal rights laws and other elements of a comprehensive legal system that is effectively, impartially and cleanly administered by a well-functioning, impartial and honest judicial and legal system." For an analysis of the new *World Bank* approach cf. Janik 2012, pp. 264–297.

[128] Buergenthal and Thürer 2009, p. 158; World Bank 1998, pp. 11–12.

[129] See Gentilini et al . 2014.

[130] World Bank 1998, pp. 5–6; cf. also Oberleitner 2007, p. 131.

[131] http://wto.org/english/docs_e/legal_e/04-wto.pdf. The preamble requests WTO Member States to make sure that "their relations in the field of trade and economic endeavour should be conducted with a view to raising standards of living", the human rights context of this provision is not addressed, however.

[132] In the *Agreement on Agriculture* (http://wto.org/english/docs_e/legal_e/14-ag.pdf) several provision take into account issues of food security, and the GATT (http://wto.org/english/docs_e/legal_e/06-gatt.pdf) in its Article XX lit.(b) offers WTO Members the possibility to implement trade restrictions to protect human life and human health, but again the reference to relevant social rights is lacking.

> … under WTO rules no country should be prevented from taking measures for the protection of human … life or health.

The document additionally refers to the core labor standards[133] and to the issue of food security.[134] In the *Declaration on the TRIPS Agreement and Public Health*,[135] adopted by WTO Member States in Doha as an additional document against the background of the conflict between TRIPS-patent protection and the right to health, a clear reference to human rights is also avoided. This applies similarly to the document "Developmental Aspects of the Doha Round of Negotiations", tabled in 2010 by the *Committee on Trade and Development*, which repeatedly makes the issue of food security the subject of the paper,[136] but leaves unmentioned the essential human rights context.[137] Nor do the documents adopted in December 2013 in Bali, which were meant to keep the door open to a potentially successful conclusion of the *Doha Round*, contain any direct reference to the importance that international trade regulations have on the protection of social rights. The compromise—based primarily on an initiative of the Indian

[133] Para 8 *Ministerial Declaration*, WT/MIN(01)/DEC/1, 20.11.2001, http://www.wto.org/english/thewto_e/minist_e/min01_e/mindecl_e.htm. On the debate, both in international trade politics as well as in academic literature, whether or not social and labor standards are to be integrated in the international trade framework, see, for example, Spelten 2005; Kaufmann 2007; Nadakavukaren 2010, pp. 99–315; Scherrer and Hänlein 2012.

[134] Para 13 *Ministerial Declaration*.

[135] WT/MIN(01)/DEC/2, 20.11.2001, http://www.wto.org/english/thewto_e/minist_e/min01_e/mindecl_trips_e.htm.

[136] WT/COMTD/W/143/Rev.5, 28.10.2010, see, for example, Para 7: "A significant reduction in tariffs and the expansion of tariff quotas, particularly in developed country markets, is being sought by many developing countries. … At the same time, many developing countries are concerned about the likely impact of tariff reductions on rural livelihood, and consequently on their food security concerns, in particular should domestic support levels remain high in some other countries.", and Para 25: "Issues of interest to developing countries … include … (a)ppropriate S&D (special and differential treatment) for developing countries, including the flexibility to designate an appropriate number of products as Special Products guided by indicators based on the criteria of food security, livelihood security and rural development needs, and the establishment of a Special Safeguard Mechanism."

[137] Cf. in this context also the dispute between the former UN Special Rapporteur on the Right to Food Olivier De Schutter and the former WTO General Secretary Pascal Lamy on "The World Trade Organization and the Post-Global Food Crisis Agenda. Putting Food Security First in the International Trade System", https://www.wto.org/english/news_e/news11_e/deschutter_2011_e.pdf; https://www.wto.org/english/news_e/news11_e/aGeneral Comment No.om_14dec11_e.htm; on this complex see also the statement of the UN Special Rapporteur on the Right to Food on "Trade negotiations need to reflect the new global consensus on hunger", 2.12.2009, http://www.ohchr.org/EN/NewsEvents/Pages/DisplayNews.aspx?NewsID=9656&LangID=E; furthermore the report on his mission to the World Trade Organization, UN Doc. A/HRC/10/5/Add.2, 4.2.2009, http://daccess-dds-ny.un.org/doc/UNDOC/GEN/G09/106/39/PDF/G0910639.pdf?OpenElement.

government—allowing transition and developing countries to maintain their agriculture subsidies as long as they are used to secure food supply,[138] has, inter alia, contributed to the successful completion of the conference on Bali. However, the right to food, which represents without any doubt the international legal basis for this important exemption regulation, it is not named in the relevant documents. Even though the WTO in its work, on the one hand, takes up individual development policy issues and inter alia publicly promotes its own important contribution to the achievement of MDGs,[139] its attitude with regard to the subject of "human rights" remains, on the other hand, extremely reluctant, at least according to its official statements.[140] This is indeed surprising, as liberalization of global trade—the main objective of the WTO—is without doubt not exclusively accompanied by threats to human rights: Global welfare increases which are expected to be achieved by the implementation of WTO rules should, of course, also contribute to an improvement of living conditions in poorer parts of the population in developing countries—and, thereby, protect the social rights of these people.

Taking into consideration the hardly deniable relevance of social rights for the work of international financial organizations and of the WTO, some observers consider the reflection of this importance in an adequate change of the respective legal documents as long overdue.[141] Such an amendment would not merely lead to a rhetorical appreciation of human rights issues, but would also strengthen the

---

[138] Cf. the *Ministerial Decisions on General Services* (WT/MIN(13)/37—WT/L/912) and on *Public Stockholding for Food Security Purposes* (WT/MIN(13)/38—WT/L/913); for more information see https://www.wto.org/english/news_e/news13_e/mc9sum_07dec13_e.htm#agriculture and https://www.wto.org/english/thewto_e/minist_e/mc9_e/brief_agneg_e.htm#stockholding.

[139] In particular MDG 8 (global partnership for development) is highlighted in this context, but the WTO secretariat also refers to the importance of the global trade system for other MDGs; cf. WTO, The WTO and the Millennium Development Goals, http://wto.org/english/thewto_e/coher_e/mdg_e/mdg_e.htm, p. 11: "WTO activities are also having a fundamental impact on MDG 1, which aims to eradicate poverty and hunger. While the relationship between open trade and growth is quite complex, it is widely recognized that the WTO's work is having an impact on achieving MDG 1 because open trade, accompanied by sound domestic and international policies, can lead to enhanced levels of growth and poverty reduction. Attaining MDG 1 will thus support countries in meeting their social objectives and in achieving all the MDGs." See also Bender 2007, pp. 11–25.

[140] On the question to what extent WTO dispute settlement bodies have to take into account human rights obligations of WTO members in their decisions, see Marceau 2002; Weiß 2007, Para 1108; Hörmann 2010, Para 12; Joseph 2011, pp. 50–53; Hestermeyer 2014, pp. 268–275; cf. in this context the ILA resolution 5/2008 ("Rio de Janeiro Declaration") which explicitly declares that "WTO members and bodies are legally required to interpret and apply WTO rules in conformity with the human rights obligations of WTO members under international law"; see also 8th report of the ILA-International Trade Law Committee (ITLC), Paras 35–42 (both documents are available at http://www.ila-hq.org/en/committees/index.cfm/cid/24) and Petersmann 2014.

[141] See, for the *World Bank*, Head 2008, p. 204, and, for the WTO, Feyder 2010, p. 186 (supporting stronger attention to the right to food in the WTO-*Agreement on Agriculture*). On further proposals containing a stronger linking of the WTO to human rights standards, cf. Hilf and Hörmann 2005, pp. 458–463; Orford 2006, pp. 159–192; Konstantinov 2009; Joseph 2011, pp. 265–284; cf. in this context also the debate between Petersmann 2002, 2008, Alston 2002, and Howse 2002, 2008.

mandate of these organizations and offer them the possibility to ensure, in cooperation with other international organizations—among them human rights institutions of the UN system in particular—, more substantive coherence in the global governance-architecture. However, it should not be overlooked that the legal obligation to take into account social rights in the practice of international trade law and international development finance already exists: Even though the WTO, IMF and the development banks themselves are not direct addressees of human rights treaties, the obligation under international law to respect human rights concerns in any case the Member States of these organizations. They are either the contracting parties of relevant human rights agreements or at least bound via customary international law to the fundamental human rights obligations which are covered by the UDHR. Member States, through their representatives in the committees of international organizations, therefore need to make sure that the regulatory framework of these organizations is interpreted in accordance with human rights, and that measures and decisions of the organization do not result in threats or violations of human rights.[142] As such, an "indirect commitment" of international organizations towards consideration of human rights concerns can be assumed, imparted via the members of the respective organization.[143]

The CESCR has frequently emphasized this special form of extraterritorial obligations of States for the area of social human rights, for example in its *General Comment on the Right to Social Security*:

> States parties should ensure that their actions as members of international organizations take due account of the right to social security. Accordingly, States parties that are members of international financial institutions, notably the International Monetary Fund, the World Bank, and regional development banks, should take steps to ensure that the right to social security is taken into account in their lending policies, credit agreements and other international measures. States parties should ensure that the policies and practices of international and regional financial institutions, in particular those concerning their role in structural adjustment and in the design and implementation of social security systems, promote and do not interfere with the right to social security.[144]

Nevertheless, the CESCR also places international organizations themselves under obligation, as in the same *General Comment* it is stated under the headline "Obligations of Actors other than States":

---

[142] Cogen 1992, p. 387; Dann 2012, pp. 244–245; Narula 2013, pp. 131–135; Hestermeyer 2014, pp. 264–265.

[143] Hörmann 2010, Para 10.

[144] CESCR 2008, Para 58. Similar wordings can be found for example in CESCR 2000, Para 39; cf. also CESCR 1999b, Para 8: "The Committee urges WTO members to ensure that their international human rights obligations are considered as a matter of priority in their negotiations which will be an important testing ground for the commitment of States to the full range of their international obligations. The Committee would welcome the opportunity to collaborate with WTO on these matters and thereby be active partners towards the realization of all the rights set forth in the International Covenant on Economic, Social and Cultural Rights."

> The United Nations specialized agencies and other international organizations concerned with social security, such as ILO, WHO, the United Nations Food and Agriculture Organization, the United Nations Children's Fund, the United Nations Human Settlements Programme, the United Nations Development Programme and ISSA, as well as international organizations concerned with trade such as the World Trade Organization, should cooperate effectively with States parties, building on their respective expertise, in relation to the implementation of the right to social security.[145] The international financial institutions, notably the International Monetary Fund and the World Bank, should take into account the right to social security in their lending policies, credit agreements, structural adjustment programmes and similar projects, so that the enjoyment of the right to social security, particularly by disadvantaged and marginalized individuals and groups, is promoted and not compromised.[146]

The *Maastricht Principles* also primarily focus on the human rights responsibility of States that must be borne via their representatives in the committees of the respective organizations. In addition, however, they highlight that the organizations can be direct addressees of human rights obligations:

> As a member of an international organization, the State remains responsible for its own conduct in relation to its human rights obligations within its territory and extraterritorially. A State that transfers competences to, or participates in, an international organization must take all reasonable steps to ensure that the relevant organization acts consistently with the international human rights obligations of that State.[147] The present Principles apply to States without excluding their applicability to the human rights obligations of international organizations under, inter alia, general international law and international agreements to which they are parties.[148]

The slightly stricter linguistic version chosen by the authors of the *Maastricht Principles*, compared to the *General Comments* ("A State … must take all reasonable steps …") corresponds indeed with the *status quo* of international law, because no reasonable grounds could be found as to why a State, in its function as a member of an international organization, should submit to different international law commitments than those it has to respect otherwise. This means that the States Parties to the ICESCR, irrespective of whether they participate in global political activities individually or by their engagement in international organizations, are bound by international law to respect social rights at the global level, to protect them from violations caused by third parties, and furthermore to aim at the implementation of social rights within their own capabilities. At least the obligations to respect and protect, which arise within the operation of international organizations, are sufficiently precise to establish concrete relations of responsibility: When international organizations make decisions that might imply a violation of these obligations, those States that have participated in the resolution are responsible for the human rights violations resulting from it. It is more difficult, however, to specify the extraterritorial obligations to fulfil, as the issue of

---

[145] CESCR 2008, Para 82.

[146] CESCR 2008, Para 83.

[147] Principe 15 *Maastricht Principles*; cf. in this context also Principle 29 *Maastricht Principles*.

[148] Principle 16 *Maastricht Principles*.

responsibility attribution in the relation between the individual addressees of obligations arises—as with international obligations to fulfil in general, which are to be considered in the context of development cooperation.[149] Again, a mere procedural obligation can be derived from the ICESCR, as the authors of the *Maastricht Principles* stated by requiring States in Principle 30

> (to) coordinate with each other, including in the allocation of responsibilities, in order to cooperate effectively in the universal fulfilment of economic, social and cultural rights.

References

Alston Ph (2002) Resisting the merger and acquisition of human rights by trade law. A reply to Petersmann. EJIL 13:815–844

Alston Ph (2005) Ships Passing in the Night. The Current State of The Human Rights and Development Debate seen through the lens of the Millennium Development Goals. HRQ 25:755–829

Alston Ph, Goodman R (2013) International human rights, 3rd edn. Oxford University Press, Oxford

Alston Ph, Quinn G (1987) The Nature and Scope of States Parties' Obligations under the International Covenant on Economic, Social and Cultural Rights. HRQ 9:156–229

Andreassen B et al (1988) Human Rights Performance in Developing Countries. The Case for a Minimal Threshold Approach. In: Andreassen B et al (eds) Human Rights in Developing Countries. Akademisk Forlag, Copenhague, pp 333–356

Apodaca C (2007) Measuring the Progressive Realization of Economic and Social Rights. In: Hertel Sh, Minkler L (eds) Economic rights. Conceptual, measurement, and policy issues. Cambridge University Press, Cambridge, pp 165–181

Bantekas I, Oette L (2013) International Human Rights Law and Practice. Cambridge University Press, Cambridge

Bender D (2007) WTO und Millennium Development Goals. Wirkt Handelsliberalisierung armutsmindernd? In: Meyer G (ed) Entwicklung durch Handel? Die Dritte Welt in der Globalisierung. Interdisziplinärer Arbeitskreis Dritte Welt, Mainz, pp 11–25

Bilchitz D (2003) Towards a reasonable approach to the minimum core. Laying the foundations for future socio-economic rights jurisprudence. S Afr J Hum Rights 19:1–26

Bilchitz D (2007) Poverty and fundamental rights. The justification and enforcement of socio-economic rights. Oxford University Press, Oxford

Bonilla Maldonado D (ed) (2013) Constitutionalism of the Global South. The Activist Tribunals of India, South Africa, and Colombia. Cambridge University Press, Cambridge

Buergenthal Th, Thürer D (2009) Menschenrechte. Ideale, Instrumente, Institutionen. Nomos, Baden-Baden

Brand D, Russell S (eds) (2002) Core obligations: building a framework for economic, social and cultural rights. Intersentia, Antwerp

Brown DK (2012) Labour standards and Human Rights. In: Narlikar A et al (eds) The Oxford handbook on the World Trade Organization. Oxford University Press, Oxford, pp 697–718

Cogen M (1992) Human rights, prohibition of political activities and the lending-policies of World Bank and International Monetary Fund. In: Chowdhury S et al (eds) The right to development in international law. Nijhoff, Dordrecht, pp 379–396

149 See supra Sect. 3.3.

Coomans F (2006) Justiciability of economic and social rights. Experiences from domestic systems. Intersentia, Antwerp

Coomans F (2007) Application of the International Covenant on Economic, Social and Cultural Rights in the Framework of International Organizations, Max Planck Yearb United Nations Law 11:369–390

Coomans F (2011) The extraterritorial scope of the international convenant on economic, social and cultural rights in the work of the United Nations Committee on Economic, Social and Cultural Rights. HRLR 11:1–35

Coomans F (2012) Die Verortung der Maastrichter Prinzipien zu den extraterritorialen Staatenpflichten im Bereich der wirtschaftlichen, sozialen und kulturellen Rechte. Zeitschrift für Menschenrechte 6:27–47

Corkery A, Way SA (2012) Integrating Quantitative and Qualitative Tools to Monitor the Obligation to Fulfil Economic, Social and Cultural Rights: the OPERA Framework. Nord J Hum Rights 30:324–349

Correa C (2003) TRIPS and Access to Drugs: Toward a Solution for Developing Countries without Manufacturing Capacity? Emory Int Law Rev 17:389–406

Cottier Th et al (eds) (2005) Human Rights and International Trade. Oxford University Press, Oxford

Courtis Ch (2006) Judicial enforcement of social rights. Perspectives from Latin America. In: Gargarella R et al (eds) Courts and social transformation in new democracies. Ashgate, Aldershot, pp 169–184

Craven MCR (1995) The International Covenant on Economic, Social and Cultural Rights—A Perspective on its Development. Clarendon Press, Oxford

Cullet Ph (2003) Patents and Medicines. The Relationship between TRIPS and the Human Right to Health. Int Aff 79:139–160

Dann Ph (2010) Solidarity and the Law of Development Cooperation. In: Wolfrum R, Kojima Ch (eds) Solidarity: A Structural Principle of International Law. Springer, Heidelberg, pp 55–78

Dann Ph (2012) Entwicklungsverwaltungsrecht. Theorie und Dogmatik des Rechts der Entwicklungszusammenarbeit, untersucht am Beispiel der Weltbank, der EU und der Bundesrepublik Deutschland. Mohr Siebeck, Tübingen (English version 2013: the law of development cooperation. A comparative analysis of the World Bank, the EU and Germany. Cambridge University Press, Cambridge)

Darrow M (2003) Between Light and Shadow. The World Bank, the International Monetary Fund and International Human Rights Law. Hart, Oxford

De Schutter O (2010) International Human Rights Law. Cases, Materials, Commentary. Cambridge University Press, Cambridge

de la Vega C et al (2011) Holding Businesses Accountable for Human Rights Violations. Recent Developments and Next Steps, FES International Policy Analysis. http://library.fes.de/pdf-files/iez/08264.pdf

De Schutter O et al (2012) Commentary to the Maastricht Principles on Extraterritorial Obligations of States in the area of Economic, Social and Cultural Rights. HRQ 34:1084–1169

De Schutter O (2014) Corporations and Economic, Social, and Cultural Rights. In: Riedel et al (eds) Economic, Social, and Cultural Rights in International Law. Contemporary Issues and Challenges. Oxford University Press, Oxford, pp 193–224

den Heijer M, Lawson R (2013) Extraterritorial Human Rights and the Concept of 'Jurisdiction'. In: Langford M et al (eds) Global Justice, State Duties. The Extraterritorial Scope of Economic, Social, and Cultural Rights in International Law. Cambridge University Press, Cambridge, pp 153–191

Donati F, Vidar M (2008) International Legal Dimensions of the Right to Food. In: Kent G (ed) Global obligation for the right to food. Rowman & Littlefield Publ, Plymouth, pp 47–88

Dowell-Jones M (2004) Contextualising the International Covenant on Economic, Social and Cultural Rights. Assessing the Economic Deficit. Nijhoff, Leiden

Drache D, Jacobs LA (eds) (2014) Linking Global Trade and Human Rights. New Policy Space in Hard Economic Times. Cambridge University Press, New York

Dreyfuss RC (2010) TRIPS and Essential Medicines. Must one size fit all? Making the WTO responsive to the global health crisis. In: Pogge Th et al (eds) Incentives for Global Public Health: Patent Law and Access to Essential Medicines. Cambridge University Press, Cambridge, pp 35–55

Eckstein SE, Wickham-Crowley TP (eds) (2003) Struggles for social rights in Latin America. Routledge, New York

Eide A (1984) The International Human Rights System. In: Eide A et al (eds) Food as a human right. United Nations University, Tokyo, pp 152–161

Eide A (2000) Universalization of human rights versus globalization of economic power. In: Coomans F et al (eds) Rendering justice to the vulnerable. Liber amicorum in honour of Theo van Boven. Kluwer Law International, The Hague, pp 99–119

Eide A (2001) Economic, social and cultural rights as human rights. In: Eide A et al (eds) Economic, social and cultural rights. A textbook, 2nd edn. Nijhoff, Dordrecht, pp 9–28

Elsig M, Dupont C (2012) Persistent deadlock in multilateral trade negotiations: the case of Doha. In: Narlikar A et al (eds) The Oxford handbook on the World Trade Organization. Oxford University Press, Oxford, pp 587–606

Ely Yamin A (2006) Derechos económicos, sociales y culturales en América Latina. Del invento a la herramienta. Plaza y Valdés, México

Emmerich-Fritsche A (2007) Zur Verbindlichkeit der Menschenrechte für transnationale Unternehmen. AVR 45:541–565

Erixon F (2014) After the Bali agreement. Lessons from the Doha Round for the WTO's post-Bali agenda. ECIPE (European Centre for international Political Economy) 2/2014. http://www.ecipe.org/publications/after-bali-agreement-lessons-doha-round-wtos-post-bali-agenda/

Felbermayr G et al (2014) Bali-Abkommen: Wer gewinnt, und wer trägt die Kosten? Ifo-Schnelldienst 67/3:3–34

Feyder J (2010) Mordshunger. Wer profitiert vom Elend der armen Länder? Westend, Frankfurt a.M.

Fujita S (2013) The World Bank, Asian Development Bank and human rights. Developing standards of transparency, participation and accountability. Elgar, Cheltenham

Gauri V, Brinks DM (eds) (2008) Courting social justice. Judicial enforcement of social and economic rights in the developing world. Cambridge University Press, Cambridge

Gentilini U et al (2014) The state of social safety nets 2014. World Bank Group, Washinton, D.C. http://www-wds.worldbank.org/external/default/WDSContentServer/WDSP/IB/2014/05/12/000350881_20140512111223/Rendered/PDF/879840WP0FINAL00Box385208B00PUBLIC0.pdf

Germanwatch, Misereor (eds) (2014) Globales Wirtschaften und Menschenrechte. Deutschland auf dem Prüfstand. https://germanwatch.org/de/download/8864.pdf

Ghazi B (2005) The IMF, the World Bank group and the question of human rights. Transnational Publ, Ardsley

Gibney M (2013) On Terminology: Extraterritorial Obligations. In: Langford M et al (eds) Global Justice, State Duties. The Extraterritorial Scope of Economic, Social, and Cultural Rights in International Law. Cambridge University Press, Cambridge, pp 32–47

Goldmann M (2014) Staatsverschuldung und Entwicklung. In: Dann Ph et al (eds) Entwicklung und Recht. Nomos, Baden-Baden, pp 377–431

Gondek M (2009) The reach of human rights in a globalizing world. Extraterritorial application of human rights treaties. Intersentia, Antwerp

Harrison J (2007) The Human Rights Impact of the World Trade Organisation. Hart, Oxford

Harrison J (2013) Establishing a Meaningful Human Rights Due Diligence Process for Corporations. Impact Assessment and Project Appraisal, pp 107–117. http://www.tandfonline.com/doi/pdf/10.1080/14615517.2013.774718

Head JW (2008) Losing the global development war. A contemporary critique of the IMF, the World Bank, and the WTO. Nijhoff, Leiden

Hennessy R (2002) Defining States' International Legal Obligations to Cooperate for Achievement of Human Development. Human Rights in Development Yearbook 8:71–98

Herdegen M (2014) Internationales Wirtschaftsrecht, 10th edn. Beck, Munich

Hestermeyer H (2007) Human Rights and the WTO, The Case of Patents and Access to Medicines. Oxford University Press, Oxford

Hestermeyer H (2014) Economic, Social, and Cultural Rights in the World Trade Organization: Legal Aspects and Practice. In: Riedel et al (eds) Economic, Social, and Cultural Rights in International Law. Contemporary Issues and Challenges. Oxford University Press, Oxford, pp 260–285

Hilf M, Hörmann S (2005) Die WTO—eine Gefahr für die Verwirklichung von Menschenrechten? AVR 43:397–465

Hilpold P (2007) Human rights and WTO law. From conflict to coordination. AVR 45:484–516

Hörmann S (2010) WTO und Menschenrechte. In: Hilf M, Oeter St (eds) WTO-Recht. Rechtsordnung des Welthandels, 2nd edn. Nomos, Baden-Baden, § 27

Howse R (2002) Human Rights in the WTO: Whose Rights, What Humanity? Comment on Petersmann. EJIL 13:651–659

Howse R (2008) Human Rights, International Economic Law and Constitutional Justice: A Reply. EJIL 19:945–953

Howse R, Teitel RG (2009) Beyond the divide: the International Covenant on Economic, Social and Political Rights and the World Trade Organization. In: Joseph S et al (eds) The World Trade Organization and Human Rights. Interdisciplinary Perspectives. Edward Elgar Publ, Cheltenham, pp 39–68

Huarte Melgar B et al (2011) The 2011 update of the OECD Guidelines for Multinational Enterprises. Balanced Outcome or an Opportunity Missed?, Beiträge zum Transnationalen Wirtschaftsrecht, vol 112, Halle. http://telc.jura.uni-halle.de/sites/default/files/BeitraegeTWR/Heft112_0.pdf

Hunt P, MacNaughton G (2007) A human rights-based approach to health indicators. In: Baderin MA, McCorquodale R (eds) Economic, social and cultural rights in action. Oxford University Press, Oxford, pp 303–330

Ibe S (2010) Implementing economic, social and cultural rights in Nigeria: Challenges and opportunities. Afr Hum Rights Law J 10:197–211

Jägers N (2011) UN guiding principles on business and human rights. Making headway towards real corporate accountability? NQHR 29:159–163

Janik C (2012) Die Bindung internationaler Organisationen an internationale Menschenrechtsstandards. Eine rechtsquellentheoretische Untersuchung am Beispiel der Vereinten Nationen, der Weltbank und des Internationalen Währungsfonds. Mohr Siebeck, Tübingen

Jawara F, Kwa A (2003) Behind the Scenes at the WTO. The real world of international trade negotiations. Zed Books, New York

Joseph S et al (2009) The World Trade Organization and Human Rights. Interdisciplinary perspectives. Edward Elgar Publ, Cheltenham

Joseph S (2011) Blame it on the WTO? A Human Rights Critique. Oxford University Press, Oxford

Kälin W, Künzli J (2009) The Law of International Human Rights Protection. Oxford University Press, Oxford

Kämpf A, Winkler I (2012) Zwischen Menschenrechtsförderung und Duldung von Menschenrechtsverletzunge? Anforderungen an die Entwicklungszusammenarbeit aus der Perspektive der extraterritorialen Staatenpflichten. Zeitschrift für Menschenrechte 6:63–94

Kaltenborn M, Norpoth J (2014) Globale Standards für soziale Unternehmensverantwortung—Corporate Social Responsibility (CSR)-Leitlinien als neue Regelungsebene des Internationalen Wirtschaftsrechts. Recht der Internationalen Wirtschaft (RIW) 60:402–410

Kaufmann Ch (2007) Globalisation and labour rights. The conflict between core labour rights and international economic law. Hart, Oxford

Khalfan A (2013) Division of Responsibility amongst States. In: Langford M et al (eds) Global Justice, State Duties. The Extraterritorial Scope of Economic, Social, and Cultural Rights in International Law. Cambridge University Press, Cambridge, pp 299–331

Klee K (2000) Die progressive Verwirklichung wirtschaftlicher, sozialer und kultureller Menschenrechte. Eine Interpretation von Article 2 Abs. 1 des Internationalen Pakts für wirtschaftliche, soziale und kulturelle Rechte. Boorberg, Stuttgart

Konstantinov B (2009) Human Rights and the WTO: Are They Really Oil and Water? JWT 43:317–338

Köster C (2010) Die völkerrechtliche Verantwortlichkeit privater (multinationaler) Unternehmen für Menschenrechtsverletzungen. Duncker & Humblot, Berlin

Kothari J (2007) Social Rights Litigation in India. Developments of the last Decade. In: Barak-Erez D, Gross AM (eds) Exploring social rights. Between theory and practice. Hart, Oxford, pp 172–192

Kradolfer M (2012) Verpflichtungsgrad sozialer Menschenrechte. Handlungsspielräume der nationalen Sozialpolitik vor dem Hintergrund von Article 9 UNO-Pakt I. AVR 50:255–284

Krajewski M (2011) Rechtliche Steuerung transnationaler Unternehmen. In: Giegerich Th (ed) Internationales Wirtschafts- und Finanzrecht in der Krise. Duncker & Humblot, Berlin, pp 35–70

Krajewski M (2014) Handel und Entwicklung. In: Dann Ph et al (eds) Entwicklung und Recht. Nomos, Baden-Baden, pp 247–285

Künnemann R (2004) Extraterritorial Application of the International Covenant on Economic, Social and Cultural Rights. In: Coomans A, Kaminga M (eds) Extraterritorial Application of Human Rights Treaties. Intersentia, Antwerp, pp 201–232

Künzli J (2001) Zwischen Rigidität und Flexibilität: Der Verpflichtungsgrad internationaler Menschenrechte. Duncker & Humblot, Berlin

Landau D (2012) The Reality of Social Rights Enforcement. HILJ 53:189–247

Langford M (ed) (2008) Social Rights Jurisprudence. Emerging Trends in International and Comparative Law. Cambridge University Press, Cambridge

Langford M et al eds (2013) Global Justice, State Duties. The Extraterritorial Scope of Economic, Social, and Cultural Rights in International Law. Cambridge University Press, Cambridge

Liebenberg S (2010) Socio-Economic Rights. Adjudication under a transformative constitution. Juta, Claremont

Manning R (2009) Using indicators to encourage development. Lessons from the millennium development goals, Danish Institute for International Studies, Copenhague. http://subweb.diis.dk/graphics/Publications/Reports2009/DIIS_Report_2009-1_Using_indicators_to_encourage_development.pdf

Marceau G (2002) WTO dispute settlement and human rights. EJIL 13:753–814

Mares R (2012) The UN guiding principles on business and human rights. Foundations and implementation. Nijhoff, Leiden

Massoud S (2013) Die Guiding Principles on Business and Human Rights. Eine absehbar begrenzte UN-Agenda. Kritische Justiz 46:7–17

Matsushita M et al (2006) The World Trade Organization. Law, Practice, and Policy, 2nd ed. Oxford University Press, Oxford

Mbazira Ch (2009) Litigating socio-economic rights in South Africa. A choice between corrective and distributive justice. University of Pretoria Law Press, Pretoria

McBeth A (2010) International economic actors and human rights. Routledge, London

McBeth A et al (2011) The International Law of Human Rights. Oxford University Press, Oxford

Mubangizi JC (2006) The Constitutional Protection of Socio-Economic Rights in Selected African Countries. A Comparative Evaluation. Afr J Legal Stud 2:1–19

Müller A (2009) Limitations to and derogations from economic, social and cultural rights. HRLR 9:557–601

Nadakavukaren SC (2010) Social regulation in the WTO. Trade policy and international legal development, Edward Elgar, Cheltenham

Narula S (2013) International Financial Institutions, Transnational Corporations and Duties of States, in: Langford M et al (eds) Global Justice, State Duties. The Extraterritorial Scope of Economic, Social, and Cultural Rights in International Law. Cambridge University Press, Cambridge, pp 114–149

Nowrot K (2003) Die UN-Norms on the responsibility of transnational corporations and other business enterprises with regard to human rights. Gelungener Beitrag zur transnationalen Rechtsverwirklichung oder das Ende des Global Compact?, Beiträge zum Transnationalen Wirtschaftsrecht, vol. 21, Halle; http: http://www.telc.uni-halle.de/sites/default/files/altbestand/Heft21.pdf

Oberleitner G (2007) Global human rights institutions. Between remedy and ritual. Polity Press, Cambridge

O'Connell P (2012) Vindicating socio-economic rights. International standards and comparative experiences, Routledge, London

Orford A (2006) Trade, human rights and the economy of sacrifice. In: Orford A (ed) International law and its others. Cambridge University Press, Cambridge, pp 156–196

Papp A (2013) Extraterritoriale Schutzpflichten. Völkerrechtlicher Menschenrechtsschutz und die deutsche Außenwirtschaftsförderung. Duncker & Humblot, Berlin

Petersmann E-U (2002) Time for a United Nations 'Global Compact' for Integrating Human Rights into the Law of Worldwide Organizations: Lessons from European Integration. EJIL 13:621–650

Petersmann E-U (2008) Human Rights, International Economic Law and Constitutional Justice: A Rejoinder. EJIL 19:955–960

Petersmann E-U (2014) International Trade Law and Human Rights: The ILA's 2008 "Rio de Janeiro Declaration. In: Bhuiyan Sh et al (eds) International law and developing countries: Essays in honour of Kamal Hossain. Brill Nijhoff, Leiden, pp 83–102

Pogge Th (2005) Recognized and Violated by International Law: The Human Rights of the Global Poor. LJIL 18:717–745

Qureshi AH (2009) International Trade for Development: The WTO as a Development Institution? JWT 43:173–188

Riegner M (2014) Entwicklungsmessung und Recht. In: Dann Ph et al (eds) Entwicklung und Recht. Nomos, Baden-Baden, pp 117–149

Robinson S (2014) International Obligations, State Responsibility and Judicial Review under the OECD Guidelines for Multinational Enterprises Regime. Utrecht J Int Eur Law 30:68–81

Roos SR (2007) Der internationale Menschenrechtsschutz vor entwicklungsbedingten Zwangsumsiedlungen und seine Sicherstellung durch Recht und Praxis der Weltbank. Duncker & Humblot, Berlin

Rudolph Ph H (2005) The Tripartite Declaration of Principles Concerning Multinational Enterprises. In: Mullerat R (ed) Corporate Social Responsibility. The Corporate Governance of the 21st Century. Kluwer, The Hague, pp 217–220

Ryngart C (2013) Jurisdiction: Towards a Reasonableness Test. In: Langford M et al (eds) Global Justice, State Duties. The Extraterritorial Scope of Economic, Social, and Cultural Rights in International Law. Cambridge University Press, Cambridge, pp 192–211

Sachs J D (2005) Das Ende der Armut. Ein ökonomisches Programm für eine gerechtere Welt. 2nd edn. Siedler Verlag, Munich (original version 2005: The end of poverty. How we can make it happen in our lifetime. Penguin Books, London)

Salomon ME (2007) Global Responsibility for Human Rights. Oxford University Press, Oxford

Salomon ME (2013) Deprivation, Causation and the Law of International Cooperation. In: Langford M et al (eds) Global Justice, State Duties. The Extraterritorial Scope of Economic, Social, and Cultural Rights in International Law. Cambridge University Press, Cambridge, pp 259–296

Saul B et al (2014) The International Covenant on Economic. Commentary, Cases and Materials. Oxford University Press, Oxford, Social and Cultural Rights

Scheinin M (2013) Core rights and obligations. In: Shelton D (ed) The Oxford handbook of International Human Rights Law. Oxford University Press, Oxford, pp 527–540

Scheper Ch (2013) The World Bank: Quo Vadis? Environmental and social safeguards under review. Global Spotlight 8/2013. http://www.sef-bonn.org/fileadmin/Die_SEF/Publikationen/GG-Spotlight/GGS_2013-08_en.pdf

Scherrer Ch, Hänlein A eds (2012) Sozialkapitel in Handelsabkommen. Begründungen und Vorschläge aus juristischer, ökonomischer und politologischer Sicht. Nomos, Baden-Baden

Schilling-Vacaflor A, Barrera A (2011) Lateinamerikas neue Verfassungen: Triebfedern für direkte Demokratie und soziale Rechte? GIGA-Focus Nr. 2; http://www.giga-hamburg.de/de/system/files/publications/gf_lateinamerika_1102.pdf

Schmucker C (2014) Doha Still the Silver Bullet. WTO's Bali agreement important development toward resolution. IP Journal April 2014. https://ip-journal.dgap.org/en/ip-journal/topics/doha-still-silver-bullet

Seibert-Fohr A, Wolfrum R (2005) Die einzelstaatliche Durchsetzung völkerrechtlicher Mindeststandards gegenüber transnationalen Unternehmen. AVR 43:153–186

Sepúlveda M (2003) The Nature of the Obligations under the International Covenant on Economic. Social and Cultural Rights, Intersentia, Antwerp

Sepúlveda M (2006) Obligations of 'International Assistance and Cooperation' in an Optional Protocol to the International Covenant on Economic, Social and Cultural Rights. NQHR 24:271–304

Sepúlveda Carmona M (2009) The obligation of 'international assistance and cooperation' under the International Covenant on Economic, Social and Cultural Rights—a possible entry point to a human rights based approach to Millennium Development Goal 8. Int J Hum Rights 13:86–109

Seufert Ph (2014) The FAO Voluntary Guidelines on the Responsible Governance of Tenure of Land, Fisheries and Forests. In: Margulis ME et al (eds) Land Grabbing and Global Governance. Routledge, London, pp 181–186

Shankar S, Mehta PB (2008) Courts and Socioeconomic Rights in India. In: Gauri V, Brinks DM (eds) Courting social justice. Judicial enforcement of social and economic rights in the developing world. Cambridge University Press, Cambridge, pp 146–182

Shawkat A et al (2011) The General Agreement on Trade in Services (GATS), water, and human rights from the perspective of developing countries. NILR 58:43–75

Shihata I (1995) The World Bank in a Changing World. Selected essays and lectures, vol II. Nijhoff, Dordrecht

Shue H (1996) Basic Rights. Subsistence, affluence and U.S. foreign policy. 2nd edn, Princeton University Press, Princeton

Skogly SI (2001) The human rights obligations of the World Bank and the International Monetary Fund. Cavendish, London

Skogly SI (2006) Beyond National Borders: States' Human Rights Obligations in International Cooperation. Intersentia, Antwerp

Skogly SI (2013) Causality and Extraterritorial Human Rights Obligations. In: Langford M et al (eds) Global Justice, State Duties. The Extraterritorial Scope of Economic, Social, and Cultural Rights in International Law. Cambridge University Press, Cambridge, pp 233–258

Skogly SI, Gibney M (2002) Transnational Human Rights Obligations. HRQ 24:781–798

Spelten W (2005) WTO und nationale Sozialordnungen. Ethische, ökonomische und institutionelle Dimensionen der Integration einer Sozialklausel in das Welthandelsrecht. Duncker & Humblot, Berlin 2005

Ssenyonjo M (2009) Economic. Social and Cultural Rights in International Law. Hart, Oxford

Stoll PT (2005) Der Zugang zu Medizin—soziale Menschenrechte und Welthandelsordnung. In: Dicke K et al (eds) Weltinnenrecht, Liber amicorum Jost Delbrück. Duncker & Humblot, Berlin, pp 739–752

Tietje Ch (2009) Begriff, Geschichte und Grundlagen des Internationalen Wirtschaftssystems und Wirtschaftsrechts. In: Tietje Ch (ed) Internationales Wirtschaftsrecht. De Gruyter, Berlin

Tietje Ch (2013) Individualrechte im Menschenrechts- und Investitionsschutzbereich—Kohärenz von Staaten- und Unternehmensverantwortung. In: Hanschel D et al (eds) Mensch und Recht. Festschrift für Eibe Riedel. Duncker & Humblot, Berlin, pp 271–288

Trilsch MA (2012) Die Justiziabilität wirtschaftlicher, sozialer und kultureller Menschenrechte im innerstaatlichen Recht. Springer, Berlin

Tully St (2001) The 2000 Review of the OECD Guidelines for Multinational Corporations. ICLQ 50:394–403

Türk E, Krajewski M (2004) Right to water and trade in services. Assessing the impact of GATS on water regulation. In: Hein W, Voegeli W (eds) GATS und globale Politik. Hamburg, Deutsches Übersee-Institut, pp 107–124

Tushnet M (2008) Weak courts, strong rights. Judicial review and social welfare rights in comparative constitutional law. Princeton University Press, Princeton

Utz B (2011) Update oder Upgrade? Eine Bilanz zur Revision der OECD-Leitsätze für multinationale Unternehmen, FES Internationale Politikanalyse. http://library.fes.de/pdf-files/iez/08232.pdf

Vagts DF (2003) The UN Norms for Transnational Corporations. LJIL 16:795–802

Vandenhole W (2003) Completing the UN Complaint Mechanisms for Human Rights Violations Step by Step: Towards a Complaints Procedure to the International Covenant on Economic, Social and Cultural Rights. NQHR 21:423–465

Vandenhole W, Benedek W (2013) Extraterritorial Human Rights Obligations and the North-South Divide. In: Langford M et al (eds) Global Justice, State Duties. The Extraterritorial Scope of Economic, Social, and Cultural Rights in International Law. Cambridge University Press, Cambridge, pp 332–363

van Genugten WJM (1992) Mensenrechten in ontwikkeling: het `goede' doel voorbij. Catholic University of Nijmegen, Nijmegen

van Genugten WJM et al (eds) (2003) World Bank, IMF and human rights. Including the tilburg guiding principles on World Bank, IMF and human rights. Wolf Legal Productions, Nijmegen

van Hoof GJH (1984) The legal nature of economic, social and cultural rights. A rebuttal of some traditional views. In: Alston P, Tomasevski K (eds) The right to food. Nijhoff, Utrecht, pp 97–110

von Bernstorff J (2011) Extraterritoriale menschenrechtliche Staatenpflichten und Corporate Social Responsibility. AVR 49:34–63

von Bernstorff J (2012a) 'Land Grabbing' und Menschenrechte: Die FAO Voluntary Guidelines on the Responsible Governance of Tenure. INEF Forschungsreihe Menschenrechte, Unternehmensverantwortung und Nachhaltige Entwicklung 11/2012. http://www.humanrights-business.org/files/landgrabbing_final_1.pdf

von Bernstorff J (2012b) Die UN Guiding Principles on Business and Human Rights. Ein Kommentar aus völkerrechtlicher Sicht. http://www.unesco.de/7390.html

von Bernstorff J, Dann Ph (2013) Reforming the World Bank's Safeguards. A Comparative Legal Analysis. GIZ, Eschborn. http://star-www.giz.de/starweb/giz/pub/servlet.starweb

Weiß W (2007) Welthandelsrecht, Menschenrechte und Sozialstandards, in: Herrmann Ch et al, Welthandelsrecht. 2nd edn. Beck, Munich, § 24

Weissbrodt D, Kruger M (2003) Norms on the Responsibilities of Transnational Corporations and other Business Enterprises with Regard to Human Rights. AJIL 97:901–922

Welling JW (2008) International indicators and economic, social, and cultural rights. HRQ 30:933–958

WHO (2006) Public health, innovation and intellectual property rights. Report of the Commission on Intellectual Property Rights, Innovation and Public Health, World Health Organization, Geneva. http://www.who.int/intellectualproperty/documents/thereport/ENPublicHealthReport.pdf?ua=1

Wilson St., Dugard J (2013) Constitutional Jurisprudence. The First and Second Waves. In: Langford M et al (eds) Socio-Economic Rights in South Africa. Symbols or Substance? Cambridge University Press, Cambridge, pp 35–62

Windfuhr M (2012) Wirtschaft und Menschenrechte als Anwendungsfall extraterritorialer Staatenpflichten. Zeitschrift für Menschenrechte 6:95–119

Windfuhr M (2013) Monitoring der Umsetzung von wirtschaftlichen, sozialen und kulturellen Menschenrechten. In: Hanschel D et al (eds) Mensch und Recht. Festschrift für Eibe Riedel. Duncker & Humblot, Berlin, pp 351–370

World Bank (1998) Development and Human Rights: The Role of the World Bank. World Bank, Washington. http://siteresources.worldbank.org/BRAZILINPOREXTN/Resources/3817166-1185895645304/4044168-1186409169154/08DHR.pdf
Xiong P (2012) An international law perspective on the protection of human rights in the TRIPS agreement. An interpretation of the TRIPS agreement in relation to the right to health. Nijhoff, Leiden
Yamane H (2011) Interpreting TRIPS. Globalisation of intellectual property rights and access to medicines. Hart, Oxford
Young KE (2008) The Minimum Core of Economic and Social Rights: A Concept in Search of Content. Yale J Int Law 33:113–176
Ziegler J (2011) Wir lassen sie verhungern. Die Massenvernichtung in der Dritten Welt, C. Bertelsmann, Munich (original version 2011: Déstruction massive. Géopolitique de la faim. Éditions du Seuil, Paris)
Ziegler J et al (2011) The Fight for the Right to Food. Lessons Learned, Palgrave Macmillan, Basingstoke

Documents of the Committee on Economic, Social and Cultural Rights (CESCR)

CESCR (1990) General Comment No. 3 on the nature of States parties obligations (Article 2, par.1) of 14.12.1990, E/1991/23. http://tbinternet.ohchr.org/_layouts/treatybodyexternal/Download.aspx?symbolno=E%2f1991%2f23(SUPP)&Lang=en
CESCR (1992) General Comment No. 4 on the right to adequate housing (Article11 [1]) of 1.1.1992, E/1992/23. http://www.refworld.org/docid/47a7079a1.html
CESCR (1999a) General Comment No. 12 on the right to adequate food (Article 11) of 12.5.1999, E/C.12/1999/5. http://tbinternet.ohchr.org/_layouts/treatybodyexternal/Download.aspx?symbolno=E%2fC.12%2f1999%2f5&Lang=en
CESCR (1999b) Statement to the Third Ministerial Conference of the World Trade Organization (Seattle, 30 November to 3 December 1999), E/C.12/1999/11 Annex VII. http://tbinternet.ohchr.org/_layouts/treatybodyexternal/Download.aspx?symbolno=E%2fC.12%2f1999%2f11&Lang=en
CESCR (2000) General Comment No. 14 on the right to the highest attainable standard of health (Article 12) of 11.8.2000, E/C.12/2000/4. http://tbinternet.ohchr.org/_layouts/treatybodyexternal/Download.aspx?symbolno=E%2fC.12%2f2000%2f4&Lang
CESCR (2001) Statement on Poverty and the ICESCR, of 10 May 2001, E/C.12/2001/10. http://tbinternet.ohchr.org/_layouts/treatybodyexternal/Download.aspx?symbolno=E%2fC.12%2f2001%2f10&Lang=enStatement on poverty
CESCR (2003) General Comment No. 15 on the right to water (Arts. 11 and 12) of 20.1.2003, E/C.12/2002/11. http://tbinternet.ohchr.org/_layouts/treatybodyexternal/Download.aspx?symbolno=E%2fC.12%2f2002%2f11&Lang=en
CESCR (2007), An Evaluation of the Obligation to take Steps to the "Maximum of its Available Resources" under an Optional Protocol to the Covenant, E/C.12/2007/1. http://tbinternet.ohchr.org/_layouts/treatybodyexternal/Download.aspx?symbolno=E%2fC.12%2f2007%2f1&Lang=en
CESCR (2008) General Comment No. 19 on the right to social security (Article 9) of 4.2.2008, E/C.12/GC/19. http://tbinternet.ohchr.org/_layouts/treatybodyexternal/Download.aspx?symbolno=E%2fC.12%2fGC%2f19&Lang=en
CESCR (2009) General Comment No. 20 on Non-discrimination in economic, social and cultural rights of 2.7.2009, E/C.12/GC/20. http://tbinternet.ohchr.org/_layouts/treatybodyexternal/Download.aspx?symbolno=E%2fC.12%2fGC%2f20&Lang=en

Chapter 4
Scope and Relevance of Specific Social Rights for Poverty Reduction Strategies in Developing and Emerging Countries

Abstract Both the UDHR and the ICESCR contain only a short listing of social rights and do not reveal much about the concrete content of those rights. The following section will cover a more intensive discussion as regards the substantive human rights in the center of the global debate on poverty—the right to an adequate standard of living (Sect. 4.1), the right to health (Sect. 4.2) and the right to social security (Sect. 4.3). The main sources of analysis are the respective *General Comments* that were drafted by the CESCR in recent years, aiming to state more precisely the individual obligations of the conventions. In addition to that, relevant *soft law* documents of international organizations have an increasing influence on the interpretation of social rights. In general, important progress has been made in the last two decades, with regard to the concretization of the most crucial social rights in international and constitutional law; however, their implementation into political practice remains deficient.

Keywords Right to food · Right to water · Right to housing · Right to health · Right to social security · Informal sector · Millennium Development Goals (MDGs)

4.1 The Right to an Adequate Standard of Living—Access to Food, Water and Adequate Housing

The extent of global poverty becomes most obvious when we consider that many people today still suffer from hunger, fall ill due to malnutrition, have insufficient access to clean water, are unable to dress adequately or simply live in the streets. The satisfaction of these basic needs, which are grouped as the so-called right to an adequate standard of living (Article 11 ICESCR)[1], is not ensured in many parts of

[1] For an overview of the protection of the family, mothers, children and young persons (Article 10 ICESCR), which can also be attributed to the catalogue of social human rights, see Saul et al. 2014, pp. 721–860.

M. Kaltenborn, *Social Rights and International Development*,
SpringerBriefs in Law, DOI 10.1007/978-3-662-45352-0_4

the world—without any doubt, poverty is also a widespread problem in "rich", industrialized countries,[2] but people in developing countries and emerging economies are of primary concern.

4.1.1 The Right to Food

The most serious development disparities between the North and the South are manifested in the realization of the right to food: According to estimations by FAO, 12.3 % of the world's population (approximately 868 million people) is malnourished, of which sub-Saharan Africa and South Asia are particularly affected.[3] The food price crisis of 2007/2008 alone has led to additional 75 million people starving worldwide.[4] Even though some progress has been made in the meantime, the international community is far away from reaching MDG target 1.C, which aims to halve the proportion of people suffering from hunger between 1990 and 2015.[5]

The question of whether people have access to sufficient food is not merely a regional or national supply problem, in this context. Only recently, when the global public was made aware of major fluctuations of staple food prices, due to gambling on the stock exchange,[6] has it become clear that the extent of the food security problem of particular developing countries should be seen in the global context. Further examples of the globalization of the food security problem are the reallocation of vast agricultural land, for the purpose of producing biofuel,[7] and the phenomenon of increasing foreign major agricultural investments in developing countries, which is often criticized as "land grabbing" and is highly controversial in development policy.[8] But above all, world trade relations, and the fact that a few industrialized nations and their agricultural protectionism are still responsible for

---

[2] See http://www.oecd.org/social/inequality-and-poverty.htm; http://www.oecd.org/social/soc/growingunequalincomedistributionandpovertyinoecdcountries.htm. All websites cited in this chapter have been last accessed 3 September 2014.

[3] FAO 2013, pp. IX, 18 (with more detailed references to the respective regions in the world), http://www.fao.org/publications/sofa/en/.

[4] FAO 2008, pp. 8, 34.

[5] United Nations 2014, p. 12.

[6] For further information on food speculation see http://www.oxfam.org/sites/www.oxfam.org/files/ib-speculation-vs-food-security-031011-en.pdf; https://www.foeeurope.org/food-speculation; http://www.foodwatch.org/en/what-we-do/topics/speculation-with-foodstuffs/2-minute-info/; http://www.wdm.org.uk/food-speculation.

[7] For a legal assessment see Heselhaus 2009; Haugen 2010; cf. also Salomon 2013, pp. 263–266.

[8] See Cotula 2012; Rudloff 2012; von Bernstorff 2012; Golay and Biglino 2013; Margulis et al. 2014.

the biggest obstacles in the way of the fight against global hunger, remain an ongoing discussion point in the North-South divide and food security policy.[9]

The former *UN Special Rapporteur on the right to food*, Jean Ziegler, has made strong statements on the problem of world hunger. The fact that 37,000 people die of hunger every day and almost one billion people are permanently malnourished, even though agriculture has the capacity to nourish twelve billion people, which is twice the world population, clearly shows that this is not merely a matter of fate: "Every child who dies of hunger in today's world has been murdered".[10] Even when one does not share Ziegler's conclusion in its radical wording—at least from a criminal law perspective—, one must admit that he offers an incisive illustration of the extent of the problem. Not least, the sentence points to the fact that hunger is not only a severe social and political problem, but also raises a legal issue. If we assume that it is indeed practicably possible to produce sufficient food for every single human being in the world, every case of death or illness because of malnutrition represents a clear violation of international law.

The right to food,[11] as it is stipulated in the ICESCR and specified by the *Committee on Economic, Social and Cultural Rights* (CESCR) in its *General Comment No. 12*, is only realized,

> when every man, woman and child, alone or in community with others, has physical and economic access at all times to adequate food or means for its procurement. The right to adequate food shall therefore not be interpreted in a narrow or restrictive sense which equates it with a minimum package of calories, proteins and other specific nutrients.[12]

The term "adequate food" is obviously rather imprecise, and the CESCR also hints at difficulties with a more detailed definition of this criterion, as it is "to a large extent determined by prevailing social, economic, cultural, climatic, ecological and other conditions".[13] In addition, it needs to be considered that the principle of progressive realization applies to the right to food, just as the other social rights, giving Contracting States a certain leeway in their time frame within which they must fulfil their legal obligations.[14] However, the obligation remains for all Contracting States—regardless of their level of development—to fulfil at least certain core obligations. According to CESCR, two elements are part of the core content of the right to food:

> The *availability* of food in a quantity and quality sufficient to satisfy the dietary needs of individuals, free from adverse substances, and acceptable within a given culture; the *accessibility* of such food in ways that are sustainable and that do not interfere with the

---

[9] See on this subject, for example, Mechlem 2006; Paasch 2008; De Schutter 2009; Mersing 2011; Krennerich 2013, pp. 264–265.

[10] http://www.zeit.de/2011/39/CH-Streitgespraech-Ziegler-Wegelin.

[11] See, generally, Eide et al. 1984; Alston and Tomasevski 1984; Kent 2005; Mechlem 2008; Windfuhr 2010; Ziegler et al. 2011; Randolph and Hertel 2013.

[12] CESCR 1999, Para 6.

[13] CESCR 1999, Para 7.

[14] CESCR 1999, Para 14; see generally supra 3.1.

> enjoyment of other human rights.[15] … Availability refers to the possibilities either for feeding oneself directly from productive land or other natural resources, or for well functioning distribution, processing and market systems that can move food from the site of production to where it is needed in accordance with demand.[16] … Accessibility encompasses both economic and physical accessibility: Economic accessibility implies that personal or household financial costs associated with the acquisition of food for an adequate diet should be at a level such that the attainment and satisfaction of other basic needs are not threatened or compromised Economic accessibility applies to any acquisition pattern or entitlement through which people procure their food and is a measure of the extent to which it is satisfactory for the enjoyment of the right to adequate food. … Physical accessibility implies that adequate food must be accessible to everyone, including physically vulnerable individuals, such as infants and young children, elderly people, the physically disabled, the terminally ill and persons with persistent medical problems, including the mentally ill. Victims of natural disasters, people living in disaster-prone areas and other specially disadvantaged groups may need special attention and sometimes priority consideration with respect to accessibility of food. A particular vulnerability is that of many indigenous population groups whose access to their ancestral lands may be threatened.[17]

This leads to the following core obligation of Contracting States with regard to the right to food:

> Violations of the Covenant occur when a State fails to ensure the satisfaction of, at the very least, the minimum essential level required to be free from hunger. In determining which actions or omissions amount to a violation of the right to food, it is important to distinguish the inability from the unwillingness of a State party to comply. Should a State party argue that resource constraints make it impossible to provide access to food for those who are unable by themselves to secure such access, the State has to demonstrate that every effort has been made to use all the resources at its disposal in an effort to satisfy, as a matter of priority, those minimum obligations. … A State claiming that it is unable to carry out its obligation for reasons beyond its control therefore has the burden of proving that this is the case and that it has unsuccessfully sought to obtain international support to ensure the availability and accessibility of the necessary food.[18]

The international community is accordingly obliged to assist, especially in humanitarian emergency situations.[19] However, also within regular development cooperation, such as international financial institutions' lending policy, the right to food must be paid sufficient attention.[20] With this requirement, given particular

[15] CESCR 1999, Para 8.

[16] CESCR 1999, Para 12.

[17] CESCR 1999, Para 13.

[18] CESCR 1999, Para 17; see also Künnemann 2002.

[19] CESCR 1999, Para 38.

[20] CESCR 1999, Para 41. Cf. in this context Article 11(2) ICESCR, where the obligation to international cooperation for the improvement of food supply is emphasized: "The States Parties to the present Covenant, recognizing the fundamental right of everyone to be free from hunger, shall take, individually and through international co-operation, the measures, including specific programmes, which are needed: (a) To improve methods of production, conservation and distribution of food by making full use of technical and scientific knowledge, by disseminating knowledge of the principles of nutrition and by developing or reforming agrarian systems in such a way as to achieve the most efficient development and utilization of natural resources; (b) Taking into account

emphasis in the final part of *General Comment No. 12*, the CESCR responded primarily to the social problems that have had arisen in certain Third World countries as a result of the structural adjustment programmes of the IMF and the *World Bank* in the 1980s and early 1990s.[21] Meanwhile, international financial institutions have shifted towards linking their lending policies with the development and updating of *Poverty Reduction Strategy Papers*, which regularly include nutrition as a central issue.[22]

4.1.2 The Right to Water

Also, the right to access to clean water,[23] although not mentioned explicitly in the ICESCR, can be derived from the right to an adequate standard of living and the right to health according to the CESCR.[24] This right is violated massively in many parts of the world. Contaminated drinking water causes infectious diseases and diarrhea which are easy to avoid, but often lethal; missing or insufficient sanitary facilities additionally reinforce the problem. However, many things have improved here since the adoption of the *Millennium Declaration*: In MDG target 7.C the international community had envisaged halving the proportion of people without sustainable access to safe drinking water and basic sanitation by 2015. This target was reached some time ago: According to the UN, the proportion of the world population with access to improved drinking water resources has risen between 1990 and 2012 from 76 to 89 %. Nevertheless, approximately 748 million people still do not have a sufficient supply of drinking water; 173 million people even rely on rivers, creeks, ponds or lakes for their daily water needs.[25]

As with other social rights, the obligations to respect, to protect and to fulfil are also to be applied to the human right to water. In particular, the second dimension has been the subject of intense debate in recent years, as the growing tendency towards complete or partial privatization of water supply has triggered in many countries—concern about drastic rises in the cost of drinking water and on

(Footnote 20 continued)
the problems of both food-importing and food-exporting countries, to ensure an equitable distribution of world food supplies in relation to need." See for a detailed analysis of the international dimensions of the right to food Kent 2008.

21 Cf. Stiglitz 2004, p. 13.

22 See Claeson et al. 2002.

23 See Salman and McInerney-Lankford 2004; Riedel and Rothen 2006; Rudolf 2007; Laskowski 2010; Sultana 2012; Winkler 2012; Thielbörger 2014.

24 CESCR 2003, Para 3; cf. also UN-GA Res. 64/292, 28.7.2010. There is no common assessment on whether the right to water covers not only drinking water supply, but also water that is used for agricultural production, for instance. A lot of factors suggest, however, that water resources needed for agriculture are rather thematically to fall within the ambit of the right to adequate food; cf. also CESCR 2003, Para 7.

25 United Nations 2014, p. 44.

emerging supply shortages, in particular in the global South. In her report to the HRC in 2010, the *Independent Expert on the Right to Water*, Catarina de Albuquerque, highlighted the various dimensions of the topic: Not only risks, but also chances to extend and to considerably improve drinking water supply can arise from the involvement of private companies in this sector.[26] It is important that the respective government ensures, via appropriate regulating and controlling procedures, that water is available and affordable, not only for certain parts of the population, but for everyone, and that its quality is adequate. In addition, the participation of the concerned population in the selection of companies and in all phases of service provision is of crucial importance to the effective implementation of the right to water.[27] The issue has been clearly addressed in *General Comment No. 15*:

> The obligation to protect requires State parties to prevent third parties from interfering in any way with the enjoyment of the right to water. Third parties include individuals, groups, corporations and other entities as well as agents acting under their authority. The obligation includes, inter alia, adopting the necessary and effective legislative and other measures to restrain, for example, third parties from denying equal access to adequate water; and polluting and inequitably extracting from water resources, including natural sources, wells and other water distribution systems.[28] ...Where water services (such as piped water networks, water tankers, access to rivers and wells) are operated or controlled by third parties, States parties must prevent them from compromising equal, affordable, and physical access to sufficient, safe and acceptable water. To prevent such abuses an effective regulatory system must be established, in conformity with the Covenant and this General Comment, which includes independent monitoring, genuine public participation and imposition of penalties for non-compliance.[29] ... Any payment for water services has to be based on the principle of equity, ensuring that these services, whether privately or publicly provided, are affordable for all, including socially disadvantaged groups. Equity demands that poorer households should not be disproportionately burdened with water expenses as compared to richer households.[30] ... (G)ood governance is essential to the effective implementation of all human rights, including the realization of the right to water. In order to create a favourable climate for the realization of the right, States parties should take appropriate steps to ensure that the private business sector and civil society are aware of, and consider the importance of, the right to water in pursuing their activities.[31]

---

[26] UN-Doc. A/HRC/15/31 v. 29.6.2010, http://www2.ohchr.org/english/bodies/hrcouncil/docs/15session/A.HRC.15.31.Add.1_en.pdf, Para 7. Cf. in this context also the analysis of Marin 2009; Kreide and Krennerich 2010; Moyo 2012, pp. 370–379; Thielbörger 2014, pp. 145–169.

[27] Critically on the implementation of obligations to protect in case of privatizations Kothari 2006.

[28] CESCR 2003, Para 23.

[29] CESCR 2003, Para 24.

[30] CESCR 2003, Para 27.

[31] CESCR 2003, Para 49.

4.1.3 The Right to Housing

Another central component of the right to an adequate standard of living is the right to access to adequate housing,[32] which is explicitly included in this social right.[33] The CESCR dealt early with the substantiation of this basic social right. In its *General Comment No. 4*, adopted in 1991, the CESCR describes the main requirements as follows:

> In the Committee's view, the right to housing should not be interpreted in a narrow or restrictive sense which equates it with, for example, the shelter provided by merely having a roof over one's head or views shelter exclusively as a commodity. Rather it should be seen as the right to live somewhere in security, peace and dignity.[34] … (T)he concept of adequacy is particularly significant in relation to the right to housing since it serves to underline a number of factors which must be taken into account in determining whether particular forms of shelter can be considered to constitute 'adequate housing' for the purposes of the Covenant. While adequacy is determined in part by social, economic, cultural, climatic, ecological and other factors, the Committee believes that it is nevertheless possible to identify certain aspects of the right that must be taken into account for this purpose in any particular context. They include the following: (a) *Legal security of tenure*: … Notwithstanding the type of tenure, all persons should possess a degree of security of tenure which guarantees legal protection against forced eviction, harassment and other threats. (b) *Availability of services, materials, facilities and infrastructure*: … All beneficiaries of the right to adequate housing should have sustainable access to natural and common resources, safe drinking water, energy for cooking, heating and lighting, sanitation and washing facilities, means of food storage, refuse disposal, site drainage and emergency services; (c) *Affordability*: Personal or household financial costs associated with housing should be at such a level that the attainment and satisfaction of other basic needs are not threatened or compromised …; (d) *Habitability*: Adequate housing must be habitable, in terms of providing the inhabitants with adequate space and protecting them from cold, damp, heat, rain, wind or other threats to health, structural hazards, and disease vectors. … (e) *Accessibility*: Adequate housing must be accessible to those entitled to it. Disadvantaged groups must be accorded full and sustainable access to adequate housing resources. … (f) *Location*: Adequate housing must be in a location which allows access to employment options, health-care services, schools, child-care centres and other social facilities. … (g) *Cultural adequacy*: The way housing is constructed, the building materials used and the policies supporting these must appropriately enable the expression of cultural identity and diversity of housing.[35]

The problem of insufficient housing supply has also been a topic of the MDGs. According to target 7.D, a considerable improvement in living conditions of at least 100 million slum dwellers should be achieved by 2020. Already during the first decade after the adoption of MDGs, much more has been achieved than intended in the target, as more than 200 million slum dwellers have now permanent

---

[32] See Leckie 2003; Majinge 2010; Hohmann 2013.

[33] On the right to adequate clothing, also protected by Article 11 ICESCR, see Engbruch 2008, pp. 225–240; Saul et al. 2014, pp. 924–926.

[34] CESCR 1992, Para 7.

[35] CESCR 1992, Para 8.

accommodation or sufficient housing respectively; however, the relevant challenges persist since the number of urban inhabitants living in slums continues to grow in developing countries.[36] Forced displacements of the local population, for instance due to major construction projects, such as dams or establishment of industries, come continually into the focus of public interest, too. Various human rights are thereby jeopardized, in particular the right to access to adequate housing.[37]

4.2 The Right to Health

The right to health[38] is not only mentioned in all international—global and regional—treaties that contain catalogues of social rights, but is, furthermore, also the subject-matter (or at least the human rights background) of many more international legal documents that are dedicated either to global health in general or to individual specialized topics.[39] One of the most important documents in this context, the *WHO Constitution,*[40] includes a very broad definition of what should be covered by the right to health. The preamble of the *WHO Constitution* states:

> Health is a state of complete physical, mental and social well-being and not merely the absence of disease or infirmity. The enjoyment of the highest attainable standard of health is one of the fundamental rights of every human being without distinction of race, religion, political belief, economic or social condition.

Not without good reason, this description has been subject to criticism as an ultimately unattainable ideal situation, because "complete physical, mental and social well-being" for everyone cannot be guaranteed by any State in the world.[41]

---

[36] United Nations 2014, p. 46. For a detailed analysis of the challenges for housing policy in developing countries see Kajumulo Tibaijuka 2009, pp. 166–178.

[37] In this context see also Para 6 of the *Guiding Principles on Internal Displacement* (E/CN.4/1998/53/Add.2) which have been presented to the Commission on Human Rights in 1998: "(1) Every human being shall have the right to be protected against being arbitrarily displaced from his or her home or place of habitual residence. (2) The prohibition of arbitrary displacement includes displacement: (a) When it is based on policies of apartheid, 'ethnic cleansing' or similar practices aimed at/or resulting in altering the ethnic, religious or racial composition of the affected population; (b) In situations of armed conflict, unless the security of the civilians involved or imperative military reasons so demand; (c) In cases of large-scale development projects, which are not justified by compelling and overriding public interests; (d) In cases of disasters, unless the safety and health of those affected requires their evacuation; and (e) When it is used as a collective punishment. (3) Displacement shall last no longer than required by the circumstances."; see also Roos 2007, pp. 111–121; Krennerich 2013, pp. 230–234; Saul et al. 2014, pp. 933–937.

[38] See Hunt 2006; Clapham et al. 2009; Riedel 2011; Tobin 2012; Wolff 2012; Zuniga et al. 2013; Murphy 2013.

[39] For an overview see the comprehensive collection of basic international documents edited by Marks 2012.

[40] 14 UNTS 185, https://treaties.un.org/doc/Publication/UNTS/Volume%2014/v14.pdf.

[41] See Ssenyonjo 2009, p. 318 (with further references).

Furthermore, the "social well-being" status would only be attained when all social rights were entirely fulfilled—which would mean in turn that the other social rights were ultimately dispensable.[42] Although the formulation of the *WHO Constitution* has not been taken over by the ICESCR authors for the right to health,[43] the entitlement has not been defined more narrowly.[44] According to Article 12(1) ICESCR, the Contracting States recognize "the right of everyone to the enjoyment of the highest attainable standard of physical and mental health". In their *General Comment No. 14*, the CESCR members write that they are well aware of the fact

> that, for millions of people throughout the world, the full enjoyment of the right to health still remains a distant goal. Moreover, in many cases, especially for those living in poverty, this goal is becoming increasingly remote. The Committee recognizes the formidable structural and other obstacles resulting from international and other factors beyond the control of States that impede the full realization of Article 12 in many States parties.[45]

The extent of context dependency within the implementation of the right to health is also reflected in other parts of the *General Comment*. It is highlighted, for example, that

> (t)he notion of ‚the highest attainable standard of health' … takes into account both the individual's biological and socio-economic preconditions and a State's available resources. There are a number of aspects which cannot be addressed solely within the relationship between States and individuals; in particular, good health cannot be ensured by a State, nor can States provide protection against every possible cause of human ill health. Thus, genetic factors, individual susceptibility to ill health and the adoption of unhealthy or risky lifestyles may play an important role with respect to an individual's health. Consequently, the right to health must be understood as a right to the enjoyment of a variety of facilities, goods, services and conditions necessary for the realization of the highest attainable standard of health.[46]

Moreover, it is rightly pointed out in the *General Comment* that the right to health is an inclusive right indeed that is not only applicable to health care, but also on its underlying "determinants of health",

> such as access to safe and potable water and adequate sanitation, an adequate supply of safe food, nutrition and housing, healthy occupational and environmental conditions, and access to health-related education and information.[47]

---

[42] Eichenhofer 2012, p. 112.

[43] Cf. Meier 2013, p. 80.

[44] According to Bantekas and Oette 2013, p. 390, the health term of ICESCR is even broader than the term in the WHO constitution; in contrast, Steiner 2004, p. 54, comes to the opposite conclusion. On the health term discussion in international human rights law cf. also Gross 2007, pp. 292–300; Tobin 2012, pp. 121–132; Marks 2013, pp. 5–6; Saul et al. 2014, pp. 979–996.

[45] CESCR 2000, Para 5.

[46] CESCR 2000, Para 9.

[47] CESCR 2000, Para 11. The "underlying determinants of health" are also a subject-matter of the minimum core obligations; see CESCR 2000, Para 43.

Despite the difficulties that arise on the level of conceptualization and exact capture of the meaning of "health", the CESCR has sought to specify Article 12 ICESCR in ways that make it more manageable for States. In doing so, the Committee has resorted to an interpretation structure that is also applied on other social rights.[48] Medical facilities and programs must be sufficiently available and accessible for everyone in a non-discriminatory manner. In this respect, the criterion of accessibility entails, in particular, economic considerations: deprived groups and poorer households must not be disproportionately burdened with health expenditure. With regard to the criterion of acceptability, healthcare facilities must respect the state of the art of medical ethics and must be culturally appropriate. Furthermore, scientific and medical quality standards are to be complied with.[49] With regard to the tripartite structure of human rights obligations,[50] the obligation to respect is to be mentioned first; i.e. Contracting States may not, for instance, deny individual persons or groups (inter alia prisoners, persons belonging to minorities, asylum seekers or illegal immigrants) access to health service, restrict the use of traditional methods of treatment or retain certain information on health issues. In addition, the obligations to protect with regard to the right to health are to be respected: In particular, the States have to ensure through legal requirements or other political measures that privatization in the public health sector does not result in a negative impact on the healthcare of the population. When certain groups are exposed to specific health risks caused by a third party (gender-based violence is to be mentioned here in particular), the States are required to take appropriate precautions. Finally, States are also subject to the obligation to fulfil: They are responsible for the provision of sufficient public health infrastructure (hospitals and other health facilities, counselling and information services, vaccination programs, vocational training institutions for physicians and other medical staff) and also of a public, private or mixed health insurance system accessible and affordable for people. Moreover, the field of the obligation to fulfil also covers the environmental duties of the State, since different forms of pollution contribute to a large extent to the expansion of health risks.

Against the background of the broad definition of the right to health and its specific obligations, as laid down in detail in the *General Comment No. 14*, it is not surprising that the range of topics which are discussed in relation to this fundamental human right is highly diverse. Looking solely at the "Issues in focus" that have preoccupied the *UN Special Rapporteur* for the last 10 years[51] illustrates this plurality: His reports submitted to the UN human rights bodies and to the *General Assembly* concern inter alia the development of health systems,[52] the role of civil

[48] On the following see CESCR 2000, Paras 12, 30–37.

[49] For a detailed analysis of the principles of availability and accessibility with regard to the right to health see Tobin 2012, pp. 158–174.

[50] See for the right to health, inter alia Riedel 2011, Paras 34–42; Krennerich 2013, pp. 206–222.

[51] http://www.ohchr.org/EN/Issues/Health/Pages/IssuesFocus.aspx.

[52] UN-Doc. A/HRC/7/11 v. 31.1.2008; E/CN.4/2006/48 v. 3.3.2006.

society and health professionals in the fulfilment of the right to health,[53] special human rights issues on mental disabilities[54] and neglected diseases,[55] reproductive health,[56] reduction of maternal mortality,[57] violence prevention in relation to the right to health,[58] accessibility to medicines,[59] the growing importance of the issue of prioritization of health interventions in light of scarce financial resources,[60] but also the special health problems of indigenous peoples.[61]

Not all of these problems are specifically related to developing countries. Nevertheless, there is no doubt that people in developing countries suffer most from infringements of the right to health in almost all respects. Taking the MDGs as a reference, the fulfilment of the right to health seemed to be the most urgent concern for international cooperation at least at the turn of the millennium. Not less than four out of a total of eight goals show a direct link to the right enshrined in Article 12 ICESCR—also, remarkable progress has been made in all four areas since the adoption of the MDGs. The reduction of child mortality, as striven for in MDG 4, for example, has been achieved in many parts of the world: Between 1990 and 2012, the mortality rate of children under the age of five dropped globally from 90 to 41 %. Especially in East Asia and North Africa, but also in other areas of the global South, the chances of survival for children could be improved markedly. However it will probably take until 2028 to actually reach MDG 4 globally (reduction of child mortality by two thirds).[62] Still 18.000 children die every day,[63] mostly of avoidable diseases (such as pneumonia, diarrhea, malaria) or due to malnutrition.[64] In this regard, the situation in sub-Saharan Africa is particularly problematic: The continent has the highest mortality rate in the world for children under age five, and, moreover, it is the only region where the number of live births and the under-five population are expected to rise substantially over the next two decades.[65] Predictions for MDG 5 that targets a significant improvement of maternal health are similar. Progress has been made here as well—in particular (as well as with regard to MDG 4) in North Africa and East Asia, where the maternal

---

[53] UN-Doc. A/HRC/4/28 v. 17.1.2007; specifically on the problem of skills drain also UN- Doc. A/60/348 v. 12.9.2005, Paras 18–89.

[54] UN-Doc. E/CN.4/2005/51, 11.2.2005.

[55] UN-Doc. E/CN.4/2004/49, 16.2.2004, Paras 76–80.

[56] UN-Doc. E/CN.4/2004/49, 16.2.2004, Paras 7–56.

[57] UN-Doc. A/61/338, 13.9.2006, Paras 7–36.

[58] UN-Doc. E/CN.4/2004/49, 16.2.2004, Paras 81–86.

[59] UN-Doc. A/61/338, 13.9.2006, Paras 37–93.

[60] UN-Doc. A/62/214, 8.8.2007, Paras 11–32.

[61] UN-Doc. A/59/422, 8.10.2004, Paras 55–58.

[62] Data for 2012 in United Nations 2014, pp. 24–27.

[63] These are estimations for 2012, http://www.unicef.org/health/index_bigpicture.html.

[64] For an analysis to which extent human rights efforts have strengthened responses to these health issues see Baer et al. 2013.

[65] United Nations 2014, p. 25.

mortality rate could be reduced by 69 and 66 % respectively—however, the goal is much more ambitious, since it envisages a reduction of the rate by three quarters from 1990 to 2015. Therefore, necessary measures such as better access to emergency obstetrical care, perinatology by medically trained staff and last but not least the provision of antiretroviral therapies for all pregnant women who rely on it, have to be implemented much faster than has been done thus far.[66]

MDG 6 is dedicated to combating HIV/Aids, malaria and other diseases. The expansion of these diseases should be halted by 2015 and gradually inverted. Furthermore, the year 2010 has been defined as the moment when all people who need it shall have general access to HIV/Aids treatment. Despite some improvements that have been achieved in the past years, these targets have been missed: The infection rate of HIV/Aids is still much too high (2.3 million people—mainly in sub-Saharan Africa—were infected with the virus in 2012), an estimated 35.3 million people lived with HIV/Aids worldwide, but only 30 % of people in need of treatment had access to antiretroviral therapy.[67] In 2012, an estimated 1.3 million people died from tuberculosis. Approximately 207 million cases of malaria, an estimated 627,000 of them fatal, were globally counted the same year; infants are still at particularly high risk—the proportion of children under the age of five amounts to an alarming 80 % of the total malaria mortality rate.[68] Finally, MDG 7 should not be overlooked in this context, since one of its targets—as already mentioned—aims at a considerable improvement of water and sanitary supply in developing countries. The achievement of this target is a crucial condition for combating many diseases.

Most of the health-related MDGs have already been identified as key elements of the right to health by the ICESCR authors. Whereas in Article 12(1), the general entitlement which is linked with this social right ("the right of everyone to the enjoyment of the highest attainable standard of physical and mental health") is formulated, Article 12(2) lists measures that seemed of special importance to the international community already in 1966 with regard to the fulfilment of this right:

> The steps to be taken by the States Parties to the present Covenant to achieve the full realization of this right shall include those necessary for: (a) The provision for the reduction of the stillbirth-rate and of infant mortality and for the healthy development of the child; (b) the improvement of all aspects of environmental and industrial hygiene; (c) the prevention, treatment and control of epidemic, endemic, occupational and other diseases; (d) the creation of conditions which would assure to all medical service and medical attention in the event of sickness.

It is striking that only the last aspect—the improvement of general health care—is not explicitly mentioned in the MDGs and that it was not included in the list of indicators for monitoring. However, this problem is in no way less urgent than combating particularly serious diseases or ensuring the protection of certain

---

[66] United Nations 2013, p. 29.

[67] United Nations 2014, pp. 34–37.

[68] United Nations 2014, pp. 37–38.

demographic groups (e.g. children and mothers). According to ILO data, almost one third of the world population has no access at all to health facilities or service providers; for many more people, general access indeed exists, but is often unaffordable, due to a lack of sufficient social protection.[69]

Certainly, there is no shortage of international statements highlighting how important it is for the international community to solve this basic problem of global health care. One such example is the *Declaration of Alma-Ata* in 1978, in which the WHO pointed out the relevance of primary health care for the fulfilment of the right to health:

> Governments have a responsibility for the health of their people which can be fulfilled only by the provision of adequate health and social measures. A main social target of governments, international organizations and the whole world community in the coming decades should be the attainment by all peoples of the world by the year 2000 of a level of health that will permit them to lead a socially and economically productive life. Primary health care is the key to attaining this target as part of development in the spirit of social justice. … Primary health care … includes at least: education concerning prevailing health problems and the methods of preventing and controlling them; promotion of food supply and proper nutrition; an adequate supply of safe water and basic sanitation; maternal and child health care, including family planning; immunization against the major infectious diseases; prevention and control of locally endemic diseases; appropriate treatment of common diseases and injuries; and provision of essential drugs; ….[70]

These basic requirements of the fulfilment of the right to health, which correspond largely with the core obligations formulated by CESCR in the *General Comment No. 14*,[71] have been taken up recently. In 2011, the *World Health Assembly* called WHO members

> to base their national or subnational health policies, strategies and plans on the overarching goals of universal coverage, people-centred primary care and health in all policies,[72] and to continue, as appropriate, to invest in and strengthen the health-delivery systems, in particular primary health care and services, and adequate human resources for health and health information systems, in order to ensure that all citizens have equitable access to health care and services; ….[73]

[69] ILO 2010, pp. 35, 41–42.

[70] Paras V, VII (3) *Declaration of Alma Ata*, adopted at the International Conference on Primary Health Care, Alma-Ata, USSR, 6–12.9.1978, http://www.who.int/publications/almaata_declaration_en.pdf; on primary health care see also Tobin 2012, pp. 263–267; Macdonald 2007, pp. 63–76.

[71] CESCR 2000, Para 43.

[72] WHA 64.8, Strengthening national policy dialogue to build more robust health policies, strategies and plans, preamble and Para 1(2), WHA64/2011/REC/1, referring to WHO 2008; WHO 2010.

[73] WHA 64.9 Sustainable health financing structures and universal coverage, WHA64/2011/REC/1, Para 1(3); cf. in this context also WHA 58.33 Sustainable health financing, universal coverage and social health insurance, WHA58/2005/REC/1.

In the past, the ILO, in particular, has repeatedly highlighted the importance of primary health care which is accessible to all.[74] However, the *Millennium Declaration*, which is without doubt the international legal document of utmost importance for the substance of development policy, lacks an explicit request to improve general accessibility to health care in developing countries. So it seems even more important to emphasize this core content of the right to health within the framework of the *Post-2015 Development Agenda.*[75] At the same time, the close link with another social right, namely the right to social security, becomes apparent, which will be further analyzed in the following.

4.3 The Right to Social Security

Poverty and the lack of protection against illness or unemployment still rank among the most urgent social issues in many developing countries and present, therefore, a great challenge to their national social welfare systems.[76] Governments' efforts to address these problems include traditional social security programs, as well as various other forms of basic social protection.[77] Very recently, remarkable success has been achieved in several countries. Perhaps the best-known example in the area of basic social protection is the *Bolsa Família* program, initiated by the former Brazilian president Lula da Silva.[78] Established in 2003, it is a nationwide cash transfer program, which provides support for currently approximately 12 million families, albeit on the fulfilment of certain conditions (school attendance and regular medical examinations of the children). Not least due to this program, the percentage of people living in extreme poverty in the country has been significantly reduced. Likewise in other countries (including Mexico, Argentina, Chile, Zambia, South Africa, Bangladesh, Pakistan and China) remarkable progress has been made in poverty alleviation due to the implementation of cash transfer programs, which,

---

[74] See, for example, ILO 2011, Paras 119–139.

[75] Cf. also UN Doc. A/RES/67/81, 12.12.2012, Para 25: "…consideration (shall) be given to including universal health coverage in the discussions on the post-2015 development agenda in the context of global health challenges; …".

[76] The following section is based on Kaltenborn 2014, pp. 182–185.

[77] On economic and socio-political underlying issues in this thematic field see Mkandawire 2004; Dercon 2005; Barrientos and Hulme 2008; Townsend 2009; Bender et al. 2013; Surender and Walker 2013.

[78] Federal Law 10.836/2004, http://www.planalto.gov.br/ccivil_03/_Ato2004-2006/2004/Lei/L10.836.htm. For further information on this program see, for example, Hall 2013, pp. 170–172; Coutinho 2014.

as a matter of fact, clearly vary considerably in terms of particular administrative design.[79] In particular, issues relating to the conditions attached to cash transfers[80] and the definition of target groups according to certain social criteria[81] are the subject of controversy in development research and advisory practice. Some countries also forge completely new paths in the design of their aid programs: On the basis of the Indian *Mahatma Gandhi National Rural Employment Guarantee Act*, enacted in 2005,[82] all households in rural areas in India are legally entitled to a minimum of 100 days of remunerated work annually; in 2010, approximately 55 million households already participated in the program.[83] Similar public works programs have also been successfully installed in other countries.[84]

Furthermore, some governments have opted for contributory or insurance-based schemes as the means of social protection of the population. In this respect, the type of traditional social insurance which is based on the Bismarck model is chosen in most cases, but sometimes also private insurance systems[85] and, increasingly, micro insurance[86] are implemented. The particular challenge faced by social policy experts in emerging and developing countries in the creation of such insurance systems is the strikingly low rate of employment within the formal sector of the overall labor market.[87] The number of people working in the informal sector has considerably increased in recent years, especially in many African and Asian States. Those workers are small-scale self-employed, peasant farmers and agricultural workers, as well as employees in small businesses and in many non-registered companies. The vast majority of workers in the informal sector are dependent on social protection by informal networks (e.g. family unit or caste networks) in case of unemployment, sickness or retirement. When informal sector workers are integrated into State-regulated social security schemes, not only attractive incentives to

---

[79] Leisering et al. 2006, pp. 93–179; Barrientos 2007; see also Fiszbein and Schady 2009; Hanlon et al. 2010; Barrientos 2013.

[80] Javad 2011, pp. 3–4; see also Dornan and Porter 2013; Schuering and Gassmann 2013.

[81] Hanlon et al. 2010, pp. 87–100.

[82] Act No. 42 of 2005, http://nrega.nic.in/rajaswa.pdf.

[83] Cf. Ehmke 2011, p. 82; see also Khera 2011; Kothari 2014, pp. 15–16.

[84] McCord 2008; McCord and Meth 2013.

[85] Examples to be mentioned here are the private insurance systems in the health care sector in Brazil, Chile, Uruguay, Namibia, Zimbabwe and South Africa; cf. on this issue Preker et al. 2006; Doherty and McIntyre 2013; Chapman 2014; Flood and Gross 2014.

[86] Jütting 2005; Churchill 2006; Loewe 2009; Midgley and Hosaka 2011.

[87] Almost half of the worldwide working population is self-employed. In developing countries, however, the rate of self-employment is considerably higher, mainly because the extensive lack of social security makes it necessary to take up any work in order to secure one's livelihood. The majority of these people are employed in the informal sector, mostly working in non-registered small and microenterprises. However, the increase of micro and small enterprises does not necessarily negatively affect the economic development of a country, since they also do contribute to economic growth as well as to the individual quality of life; see Ostermeier et al. 2012, p. 3; cf. also, generally, on the informal economy Pellissery 2013; on the legal issues related to the problems of the informal sector see Banik 2011.

join must be offered, but also long term, reliable funding sources must be found. There are examples of countries which successfully implemented ambitious protection schemes, including elements of social insurance—in Thailand, for example, the rate of the population covered by the national health care system was raised from 40 to 95 % of the total population in only 3 years.[88] However, the population rate covered by a "traditional" social insurance is only minor; the system is mostly financed through taxation in order to be able to cover the informal sector. Another example is Ghana, whose *National Health Insurance System*, introduced in 2003, is internationally celebrated as a "success story",[89] even though it has been able, thus far, to include only 62 % of its population.[90] Here, too, financing is mainly via State contributions and only to a minor degree via contributions by insured persons, who are usually exempted from payment obligations due to their income conditions. Similar combinations of contributory and State financing were chosen in many countries in the field of pension schemes.[91] Finally in India, based on the *Unorganised Workers Social Security Act* 2008, a social insurance program has been initiated, targeting, in particular, families with members working in informal employment and with an income below the poverty line.[92] Under the umbrella of a *National Social Security Fund*, financed by the contributions of companies and employees, as well as by State subsidies, health, pension and disability insurance services should be provided in the medium term. It is not yet foreseeable whether or not the program can actually be implemented successfully across the country—if yes, this would clearly be a very important milestone towards the realization of the right to social security in South Asia.

The problem of providing social protection for workers in the informal sector is also one of the main subjects of global social policy and thus the integral issue of a number of documents of international organizations, notably of the ILO. Already in 2002, the organization took up the issue in detail and adopted a corresponding resolution which, inter alia, states the following:

> The ILO should draw upon its mandate, tripartite structure and expertise to address the problems associated with the informal economy. An approach based on decent work deficits

[88] Hughes and Leethongdee 2007, p. 1001, see also Hanvoravongchai and Hsiao 2007. Cf. generally on new developments in social protection in South East Asian countries Cook and Pincus 2014; Köhler and Chopra 2014.

[89] WHO and Providing for Health (P4H) initiative 2011; see also Kuganab Lem 2009; Schieber et al. 2012.

[90] National Health Insurance Authority, NHIA Annual Report 2009, 2010. Some non-governmental organizations assume that the level of coverage is even below these indications; see Oxfam and Action for Global Health 2011.

[91] Introductory information on the legal design of the national security systems (especially pension schemes, health, accident and unemployment insurance) is provided by the *International Social Security Association* (ISSA) on its website "Social Security Country Profiles", http://www.issa.int/country-profiles;jsessionid=735A1F8CB7E24EE9813682FA54C68959.

[92] Act No. 33 of 2008, http://labour.gov.in/upload/uploadfiles/files/ActsandRules/SocitySecurity/TheUnorganisedWoekersSocialSecurityAct2008.pdf; see also Kothari 2014, p. 10.

> has considerable merit and should be pursued. The ILO approach should reflect the diversity of situations and their underlying causes found in the informal economy. The approach should be comprehensive involving the promotion of rights, decent employment, social protection and social dialogue. The approach should focus on assisting member States in addressing governance, employment-generation and poverty-reduction issues. …[93]

The *Declaration on Social Justice for a Fair Globalization*, adopted by the *International Labour Conference* unanimously in 2008, defines the development and strengthening of measures of social protection as one of the future core objectives of the ILO, inter alia by

> the extension of social security to all, including measures to provide basic income to all in need of such protection, and adapting its scope and coverage to meet the new needs and uncertainties generated by the rapidity of technological, societal, demographic and economic changes.[94]

Although it is not stated explicitly that this topic of the *ILO Decent Work Agenda*[95] targets the informal sector, it arises from the fact that this particular sector of society is naturally furthest apart from the objective "social security to all". The ILO has again discussed the issue in its report "Social security for social justice and a fair globalization", published in 2011:

> For a long time it was assumed that in middle- and low-income countries social security coverage would increase in line with economic development; yet this expectation was to prove misplaced. In many countries, the growing incidence of informal work led to stagnant or even declining rates of coverage. As a result, the great majority of the world population still lacks access to social security coverage. While there has been some progress in the extension of social security coverage in some parts of the world, elsewhere stagnation and even contraction have occurred. With regard to the coverage of contributory benefits, these developments are closely associated with employment trends, particularly the quantity and quality of jobs available in the formal economy. Yet governments, in consultation with social partners, have an important role to play in defining which groups of the population should be covered, and which groups are outside the realm of social insurance; in implementing and enforcing these policies; in regulating private forms of provision; and in establishing and maintaining non-contributory social security schemes which can guarantee at least a minimum level of social security coverage for all. … Comprehensive social protection (coverage by all branches of social security at least at a minimum level of benefits as guaranteed by the Social Security (Minimum Standards) Convention, 1952 (No. 102)), is not a reality for the vast majority of the world's population. A minority thereof benefits from partial social security coverage (i.e. in some of the social security branches). The ultimate aim of all ILO standards is to provide comprehensive protection to as many people as possible; the intermediate aim is to provide everyone with at least a basic level of protection. Such a "social protection floor" would guarantee at least a basic level of income security at all stages of the life cycle, as well as access to essential health services.[96]

---

[93] *Resolution concerning Decent Work and the Informal Economy*, 19.6.2002, Para 35, http://www.ilo.org/public/english/standards/relm/ilc/ilc90/pdf/pr-25res.pdf.

[94] *Declaration on Social Justice for a Fair Globalization,* 10.6.2008, http://www.ilo.org/wcmsp5/groups/public/—dgreports/—cabinet/documents/genericdocument/wcms_099766.pdf, ParaI.A.(ii).

[95] http://www.ilo.org/global/about-the-ilo/decent-work-agenda/lang–de/index.htm.

[96] ILO 2011, Paras 81–82, 85.

The ILO report of 2011 is one of the main preparatory papers for the adoption of the *Social Protection Floors Recommendation.*[97] Therefore, it is not surprising that in the latter document, social protection is expanded to those people who are not employed in formal employment relationships, but also that the reduction of the informal sector is considered as a central objective.[98] Additionally, newer strategy concepts developed by other international organizations also attach great importance to the particular problems arising from the (lack of) social protection of workers in the informal sector.[99]

How, then, does international law relate to issues of social protection? As mentioned in the beginning, both the UDHR and the ICESCR explicitly guarantee the right to social security.[100] However, both documents contain only very brief statements on how this should be eventually put into practice; likewise, the regional human rights law relevant in this regard remains vague. In contrast, the treaty law of the ILO is considerably more elaborate. In particular, the *Social Security (Minimum Standards) Convention No. 102* of 1952[101] entails detailed requirements in this regard by setting up a minimum percentage of persons covered by the social protection schemes, a minimum level and duration of benefits and a maximum qualifying period for the entitlement to benefits. But at the same time, it also contains wide margins of flexibility as it e.g. allows the Member States to gradually attain universal coverage.[102] The State parties can choose to protect 50 % of all employees, or 20 % of all residents of the economically active population or 50 % of all residents. Moreover, ratifying States have to accept at least three social security branches out of the nine listed in the convention (including at least one of the following: unemployment, old age, employment injury, invalidity and survivors). So the States can choose which social security branches are most important for them and correspond to their stage of development, later on they have the possibility to add further branches. Special exceptions are provided for developing countries. Only few emerging and developing countries, however, are yet bound by this convention—no more than 50 States have declared by treaty ratification that

---

[97] *Recommendation concerning National Floors of Social Protection* (*SPF Recommendation*), Recommendation 102, http://www.ilo.org/dyn/normlex/en/f?p=NORMLEXPUB:12100:0::NO:12100:P12100_INSTRUMENT_ID:3065524:NO.

[98] Para 15 *SPF Recommendation*: "Social security extension strategies should apply to persons both in the formal and informal economy and support the growth of formal employment and the reduction of informality, …".

[99] See, for example, HLPE 2012, pp. 25, 28; World Bank 2012, pp. XVI, 11, 23 and passim.

[100] See generally on the right to social security Scheinin 2001; Lamarche 2002; Nussberger 2005; Riedel 2007; Windfuhr 2008; van Langendonck 2007; Tooze 2007; Scruggs et al. 2013; for the concept of a "right to basic social protection" see Buschmann 2013.

[101] Convention No. 102, 210 UNTS 131, http://www.ilo.org/dyn/normlex/en/f?p=NORMLEXPUB:12100:0::NO::p12100_instrument_id:312247; see Kulke et al. 2007, pp. 15–20; Nussberger 2007, pp. 108–111.

[102] For the following see http://www.ilo.org/gimi/gess/ShowTheme.do?tid=722.

they accept the minimum standards required by ILO as binding provisions under international law.

In contrast to the other social rights enshrined in the Covenant, the provision on the right to social security in Article 9 of the ICESCR is rather brief:

> The States Parties to the present Covenant recognize the right of everyone to social security, including social insurance.

Further guidance on the potential consequences of this obligation is provided by *General Comment No. 19*, which was issued in 2008.[103] This document highlights first that the open wording of Article 9 ICESCR suggests a broad interpretation of the term "social security". Measures potentially covered by this term include contributory or insurance-based schemes (such as social insurance), non-contributory schemes (such as universal or targeted social assistance schemes) as well as other forms of social security, including privately run schemes, self-help measures and community-based or mutual schemes.[104] In the following, the *General Comment* enumerates and elaborates on the single branches of social protection included in the norm. According to Paras 12–21, the following sectors are covered: health care, sickness (cash benefits provided to those incapable of working due to ill-health), old age (social security schemes providing benefits to older persons), unemployment and employment injury, family and child support, paid maternity leave, income support to persons with disabilities, as well as benefits to survivors and orphans.[105] The general legal obligations of the States Parties to the Covenant with regard to the right to social security are listed in Paras 40–42:

> While the Covenant provides for progressive realization and acknowledges the constraints owing to the limits of available resources, the Covenant also imposes on States parties various obligations which are of immediate effect. States parties have immediate obligations in relation to the right to social security, such as the guarantee that the right will be exercised without discrimination of any kind (Article 2, Para 2), ensuring the equal rights of men and women (Article 3), and the obligation to take steps (Article 2, Para 1) towards the full realization of Articles 11, Paras 1, and 12. Such steps must be deliberate, concrete and targeted towards the full realization of the right to social security.[106] ... States parties should develop a national strategy for the full implementation of the right to social security, and should allocate adequate fiscal and other resources at the national level. If necessary, they should avail themselves of international cooperation and technical assistance in line with Article 2, Para 1, of the Covenant.[107] ... There is a strong presumption that retrogressive measures taken in relation to the right to social security are prohibited under the Covenant. If any deliberately retrogressive measures are taken, the State party has the burden of proving that they have been introduced after the most careful consideration of all alternatives and that they are duly justified by reference to the totality of the rights provided

---

[103] CESCR 2008. For a comparison of the Comment with the ILO Convention No. 102 see Nussberger 2009, Para 37.

[104] CESCR 2008, Paras 4, 5.

[105] For an overview see Saul et al. 2014, pp. 694–710.

[106] CESCR 2008, Para 40.

[107] CESCR 2008, Para 41.

> for in the Covenant, in the context of the full use of the maximum available resources of the State party. The Committee will look carefully at whether: (a) there was reasonable justification for the action; (b) alternatives were comprehensively examined; (c) there was genuine participation of affected groups in examining the proposed measures and alternatives; (d) the measures were directly or indirectly discriminatory; (e) the measures will have a sustained impact on the realization of the right to social security, an unreasonable impact on acquired social security rights or whether an individual or group is deprived of access to the minimum essential level of social security; and (f) whether there was an independent review of the measures at the national level.[108]

Altogether, it can be asserted that the provisions of international law, at least as far as they can be treated as *hard law*, leave considerable discretion to States concerning the structure of their social protection systems and socio-political programs. Only the minimum standard of social security, included in the ICESCR as a core obligation, is mandatory.[109] In addition, all contracting parties of the ICESCR are bound to the principle of non-discrimination, applicable to all social rights, and to the principle of progressive realization; with regard to procedures, they must respect the additional reporting obligations of the ICESCR, in case they do not go beyond these procedural minimum requirements and accept the special control mechanisms of the *Optional Protocol*. But if relevant ILO recommendations and the *General Comment No. 19* (even though located "only" on the level of *soft law*) are included in the appraisal, the framework of international obligations becomes considerably more complex. In particular, the *Social Protection Floors Recommendation*, adopted unilaterally by ILO Member States in 2012, contains important guidelines on the design of basic national social protection schemes, as regards content, procedures and organization. Since this recommendation represents one of the key documents for the reorientation of development policy following the end of the MDG target year 2015, it will be discussed in greater detail further below (5.2).

---

[108] CESCR 2008, Para 42.

[109] See CESCR 2008, Para 59: The States Parties have "(a) to ensure access to a social security scheme that provides a minimum essential level of benefits to all individuals and families that will enable them to acquire at least essential health care, basic shelter and housing, water and sanitation, foodstuffs, and the most basic forms of education, If a State party cannot provide this minimum level for all risks and contingencies within its maximum available resources, the Committee recommends that the State party, after a wide process of consultation, select a core group of social risks and contingencies; (b) to ensure the right of access to social security systems or schemes on a non-discriminatory basis, especially for disadvantaged and marginalized individuals and groups; (c) to respect existing social security schemes and protect them from unreasonable interference; (d) to adopt and implement a national social security strategy and plan of action; (e) to take targeted steps to implement social security schemes, particularly those that protect disadvantaged and marginalized individuals and groups."

References

Alston Ph, Tomasevski K (eds) (1984) The Right to Food. Nijhoff, Dordrecht

Baer B et al (2013) Human rights-based approaches to HIV, tuberculosis, and malaria. In: Zuniga JM et al (eds) Advancing the human right to health. Oxford University Press, Oxford, pp 245–260

Banik D (ed) (2011) The Legal Empowerment Agenda. Poverty, Labour and the Informal Economy in Africa. Ashgate, Farnham

Bantekas I, Oette L (2013) International Human Rights Law and practice. Cambridge University Press, Cambridge

Barrientos A (2007) Tax-financed social security. Int Soc Secur Rev 60:99–117

Barrientos A (2013) Social assistance in developing countries. Cambridge University Press, New York

Barrientos A, Hulme D (eds) (2008) Social Protection for the Poor and the Poorest: Concepts, Policies and Politics. Palgrave Macmillan, Basingstoke

Bender K et al (eds) (2013) Social Protection in Developing Countries. Reforming Systems. Routledge, Abingdon

Buschmann L (2013) Das Menschenrecht auf soziale Grundsicherung aus Article 9 und Article 11 ICESCR. agenda Verlag, Münster

Chapman A (2014) The Impact of Reliance on Private Sector Health Services on the Right to Health. Health Hum Rights J 16:122–134

Claeson M et al (2002) Health, Nutrition, and Population. PRSP Sourcebook, World Bank, Chap. 18. http://siteresources.worldbank.org/INTPRS1/Resources/383606-1205334112622/4978_chap18.pdf

Clapham A et al (eds) (2009) Realizing the right to health. Rüffer & Rub, Zürich

Churchill CF (ed) (2006) Protecting the Poor—A Microinsurance Compendium. International Labour Office, Geneva

Cook S, Pincus J (2014) Poverty, inequality and social protection in Southeast Asia. An introduction. J SE Asian Econ 31:1–17

Cotula L (2012) 'Land Grabbing' in the Shadow of the Law. Legal Frameworks Regulating the Global Land Rush. In: Rayfuse R, Weisfelt N (eds) The challenge of food security. International policy and regulatory frameworks. Edward Elgar Publishing, Cheltenham, pp 206–230

Coutinho DR (2014) Targeting within universalism? The Bolsa Família Program and the social assistance field in Brazil. VRÜ 47:43–61

Dercon S (ed) (2005) Insurance Against Povert. Oxford University Press, Oxford

De Schutter O (2009) International Trade in Agriculture and the Right to Food. In: De Schutter O, Cordes KY (eds) Accounting for hunger. The right to food in the era of globalisation. Hart, Oxford, pp 137–192

Doherty J, McIntyre D (2013) Addressing the failings of public health systems: Should the private sector be an instrument of choice. In: Surender R, Walker R (eds) Social Policy in a Developing World. Edward Elgar Publishing, Cheltenham, pp 101–124

Dornan P, Porter C (2013) The implications of conditionality in social assistance Programmes. In: Surender R, Walker R (eds) Social Policy in a Developing World. Edward Elgar Publishing, Cheltenham, pp 155–171

Ehmke E (2011) Indien: Arbeit für alle? Das größte Beschäftigungsprogramm der Welt. Blätter für deutsche und internationale Politik 8(2011):81–88

Eichenhofer E (2012) Soziale Menschenrechte im Völker-, europäischen und deutschen Recht. Mohr Siebeck, Tübingen

Eide A et al (eds) (1984) Food as a human right. United Nations University, Tokyo

Engbruch K (2008) Das Menschenrecht auf einen angemessenen Lebensstandard. Lang, Frankfurt a.M

FAO (2008) State of Food Insecurity in the World 2008. FAO, Rome. http://www.fao.org/docrep/011/i0291e/i0291e00.htm
FAO (2013) The State of Food and Agriculture. FAO, Rome. http://www.fao.org/publications/sofa/2013/en/
Fiszbein A, Schady N (2009) Conditional Cash Transfers. Reducing Present and Future Poverty. World Bank, Washington, D.C
Flood CM, Gross A (eds) (2014) The right to health at the public/private divide. A global comparative study. Cambridge University Press, New York
Golay Ch, Biglino I (2013) Human Rights Responses to Land Grabbing. A right to food perspective. Third World Q 34:1630–1650
Gross AM (2007) The Right to Health in an Era of Privatisation and Globalisation: National and International Perspectives. In: Barak-Erez D, Gross AM (eds) Exploring social rights. Between theory and practice. Hart, Oxford, pp 289–340
Hall A (2013) Political dimensions of social protection in Brazil. In: Midgley J, Piachaud D (eds) Social protection, economic growth and social change. Goals, issues and trajectories in China, India, Brazil and South Africa. Elgar, Cheltenham, pp 166–183
Hanlon J et al (2010) Just give money to the poor. The development revolution from the south. Kumarian Press, Sterling
Hanvoravongchai P, Hsiao WC (2007) Thailand: Achieving Universal Coverage with Social Health Insurance. In: Hsiao WC, Shaw RP (eds) Social Health Insurance for Developing Countries. World Bank, Washington, D.C, pp 133–154
Haugen HM (2010) Human Rights Impact Assessment in the Context of Biofuels: Addressing the Human Right to Food and the Human Right to Water. Nordic J Hum Rights 28:20–38
Heselhaus S (2009) Biokraftstoffe und das Recht auf Nahrung. AVR 47:93–133
HLPE (2012) Social protection for food security. A report by the High Level Panel of Experts on Food Security and Nutrition of the Committee on World Food Security, Rome. http://www.fao.org/fileadmin/user_upload/hlpe/hlpe_documents/HLPE_Reports/HLPE-Report-4-Social_protection_for_food_security-June_2012.pdf
Hohmann J (2013) The right to housing. Law, concepts, possibilities. Hart, Oxford
Hughes D, Leethongdee S (2007) Universal Coverage in the Land of Smiles: Lessons from Thailand's 30 Baht Health Reforms. Health Aff 26:999–1008
Hunt P (2006) The right to health. Key objectives, themes and interventions. In: Claude RP, Weston B H (eds) Human rights in the world community. Issues and action. University of Pennsylvania Press, Philadelphia, pp 201–209
ILO (2010) World social security report 2010/11. Covering people in times of crisis. International Labour Office, Geneva. http://www.ilo.org/wcmsp5/groups/public/—dgreports/—dcomm/—publ/documents/publication/wcms_146566.pdf
ILO (2011) Social security for social justice and a fair globalization, ILC.100/VI. International Labour Office, Geneva. http://www.ilo.org/wcmsp5/groups/public/@ed_norm/@relconf/documents/meetingdocument/wcms_152819.pdf
Javad S (2011) Social cash transfers: a useful instrument in development cooperation? Potential and pitfalls. Friedrich-Ebert-Stiftung. Dialogue on Globalization. http://library.fes.de/pdf-files/iez/08046.pdf
Jütting J (2005) Von "micro-finance" zu "micro-insurance"? Zur Rolle von freiwilligen Krankenversicherungen in Niedrig-Einkommensländern. In: Ahrens H (ed) Zur Bewertung der Entwicklungszusammenarbeit. Duncker & Humblot, Berlin, pp 131–148
Kajumulo Tibaijuka A (2009) Building Prosperity. Housing and Economic Development. Earthscan, London
Kaltenborn M (2014) Soziale Rechte und Entwicklung. In: Dann Ph et al (eds) Entwicklung und Recht. Nomos, Baden-Baden, pp 149–181
Kent G (2005) Freedom from want. The human right to adequate food. Georgetown University Press, Washington, D.C
Kent G (ed) (2008) Global obligations for the right to food. Rowman & Littlefield, Lanham
Khera R (ed) (2011) The Battle for Employment Guarantee. Oxford University Press, New Delhi

Koehler G, Chopra D (eds) (2014) Development and Welfare Policy in South Asia. Routledge, London

Kothari M (2006) Obstacles to Making Water a Human Right. In: Riedel E, Rothen P (eds) The Human Right to Water. Berliner Wissenschafts-Verlag, Berlin, pp 149–160

Kothari J (2014) A social rights model for social security: learnings from India. VRÜ 47:5–21

Kreide R, Krennerich M (2010) Das Menschenrecht auf Wasser und Sanitätsversorgung: Vereinbar mit Privatisierungen im Wassersektor? Zeitschrift für Menschenrechte 4:166–175

Krennerich M (2013) Soziale Menschenrechte. Zwischen Recht und Politik. Wochenschau Verlag, Schwalbach

Künnemann R (2002) The right to adequate food: Violations related to its minimum core content. In: Brand D, Russell S (eds) Core obligations: building a framework for economic, social and cultural rights. Intersentia, Antwerp, pp 161–184

Kuganab Lem RBA (2009) A Content Analysis of the Ghana National Health Insurance Scheme. Health Policy Dev 7:23–34

Kulke U et al (2007) Changing Tides: A Revival of a Rights-Based Approach to Social Security. In: van Langendonck J (ed) The right to social security. Intersentia, Antwerp, pp 13–36

Lamarche L (2002) Social security as a human right. In: Brand D, Russell S (eds) Core obligations: building a framework for economic, social and cultural rights. Intersentia, Antwerp, pp 89–114

Laskowski SR (2010) Das Menschenrecht auf Wasser. Die rechtlichen Vorgaben zur Sicherung der Grundversorgung mit Wasser und Sanitärleistungen im Rahmen einer ökologisch-nachhaltigen Wasserwirtschaftsordnung. Mohr Siebeck, Tübingen

Leckie S (ed) (2003) National Perspectives on Housing Rights. Kluwer, The Hague

Leisering L et al (2006) Soziale Grundsicherung in der Weltgesellschaft. Monetäre Mindestversicherungssystem in den Ländern des Südens und des Nordens. Transcript, Bielefeld

Loewe M (2009) Soziale Sicherung, informeller Sektor und das Potenzial von Kleinstversicherungen. Nomos, Baden-Baden

Macdonald ThH (2007) The Global Human Right to Health—dream or possibility? Radcliffe Publ, Oxford

Majinge Ch (2010) Right to Housing, International Protection. In: Wolfrum R (ed) Max Planck Encyclopedia of Public International Law. Oxford University Press, Oxford. http://opil.ouplaw.com/view/10.1093/law:epil/9780199231690/law-9780199231690-e2053?rskey=2js7O2&result=1&prd=EPIL

Margulis ME et al (eds) (2014) Land Grabbing and Global Governance. Routledge, London

Marin Ph (2009) Public-Private Partnerships for Urban Water Utilities: A Review of Experiences in Developing Countries. World Bank, Washington, D.C

Marks St P (2012) Health and Human Rights: Basic International Documents, 3rd edn. Harvard University Press, Cambridge

Marks St P (2013) The Emergence and Scope of the Human Right to Health. In: Zuniga JM et al (eds) Advancing the Human Right to Health. Oxford University Press, Oxford, pp 3–24

McCord A (2008) The Social Protection Function of Short-Term Public Works Programmes in the Context of Chronic Poverty. In: Barrientos A/Hulme D (eds) Social Protection for the Poor and the Poorest: Concepts, Policies and Politics. Palgrave Macmillan, Basingstoke, pp 160–189

McCord A, Meth Ch (2013) Work and welfare in the global south: public works programmes as an instrument of social policy. In: Surender R, Walker R (eds) Social Policy in a Developing World. Edward Elgar Publishing, Cheltenham, pp 172–182

Mechlem K (2006) Trade in Agriculture and Human Rights: Options for the Integration of the Right to Food into the Agreement on Agriculture. Max Planck Yearb United Nations Law 10:127–190

Mechlem K (2008) Right to Food, International Protection. In: Wolfrum R (ed) Max Planck Encyclopedia of Public International Law. Oxford University Press, Oxford. http://opil.ouplaw.com/view/10.1093/law:epil/9780199231690/law-9780199231690-e800#law-9780199231690-e800-div1-5

Meier BM (2013) The political evolution of health as a human right. Conceptualizing public health under international law, (1940s–1990s). In: Mold A, Reubi D (eds) Assembling health rights in global context. Genealogies and anthropologies. Routledge, London, pp 73–93

Mersing J (2011) How to Phase Out Rich Country Agricultural Subsidies Without Increasing Hunger in the Developing World. In: De Schutter O, Cordes KY (eds) Accounting for hunger. The right to food in the era of globalisation. Hart, Oxford, pp 193–210

Midgley J/Hosaka M eds (2011) Grassroots Social Security in Asia. Mutual Aid, Microinsurance and Social Welfare. Routledge, London

Mkandawire T (ed) (2004) Social Policy in a Development Context. Palgrave Macmillan, Basingstoke

Moyo K (2012) Privatisation of the Commons: Water as a Right; Water as a Commodity. In: Liebenberg S, Quinot G (eds) Law and Poverty. Perspectives from South Africa and Beyond. Juta, Claremont, pp 362–380

Murphy Th (2013) Health and human rights. Hart, Oxford

Nussberger A (2005) Sozialstandards im Völkerrecht. Eine Studie zu Entwicklung und Bedeutung der Normsetzung der Vereinten Nationen, der Internationalen Arbeitsorganisation und des Europarats zu Fragen des Sozialschutzes. Duncker & Humblot, Berlin

Nussberger A (2007) Evaluating the ILO's Approach to Standard-Setting and Monitoring in the Field of Social Security. In: Riedel E (ed) Social Security as a Human Right. Drafting a General Comment on Article 9 ICESCR—Some Challenges. Springer, Berlin, pp 103–115

Nussberger A (2009) Right to social security, International protection. In: Wolfrum R (ed) Max Planck Encyclopedia of Public International Law. Oxford University Press, Oxford. http://opil.ouplaw.com/view/10.1093/law:epil/9780199231690/law-9780199231690-e987?rskey=dDbnLN&result=1&prd=EPIL

Ostermeier M et al (2012) Beschäftigung, Armut und die Millenniumsziele der Vereinten Nationen. GIGA Focus Nr. 10. http://www.giga-hamburg.de/de/system/files/publications/gf_global_1210.pdf

Oxfam, Action for Global Health (2011) Achieving a Shared Goal: Free Universal Health Care in Ghana. http://www.oxfam.org/sites/www.oxfam.org/files/rr-achieving-shared-goal-healthcare-ghana-090311-en.pdf

Paasch A (2008) Weltagrarhandel und Menschenrechte – Fallstudien zu Verletzungen des Rechts auf Nahrung von Kleinbauern, Zeitschrift für Menschenrechte 2: 100–116

Pellissery S (2013) The informal economy: dilemmas and policy responses. In: Surender R, Walker R (eds) Social Policy in a Developing World. Edward Elgar Publishing, Cheltenham, pp 81–100

Preker AS et al (eds) (2006) Private Voluntary Health Insurance in Development. Friend or Foe? World Bank, Washington, D.C

Randolph S, Hertel Sh (2013) The Right to Food: A Global Perspective. In: Minkler L (ed) The State of Economic and Social Human Rights. A Global Overview. Cambridge University Press, Cambridge, pp 21–60

Riedel E (ed) (2007) Social Security as a Human Right. Drafting a General Comment on Article 9 ICESCR—Some Challenges. Springer, Berlin

Riedel E (2011) Right to Health, International Protection. In: Wolfrum R (ed) Encyclopedia of Public International Law. Oxford University Press, Oxford. http://opil.ouplaw.com/view/10.1093/law:epil/9780199231690/law-9780199231690-e806?rskey=bGghOj&result=3&prd=EPIL

Riedel E, Rothen P (eds) (2006) The Human Right to Water. Berliner Wissenschafts-Verlag, Berlin

Roos St R (2007) Der internationale Menschenrechtsschutz vor entwicklungsbedingten Zwangsumsiedlungen und seine Sicherstellung durch Recht und Praxis der Weltbank. Duncker & Humblot, Berlin

Rudloff B (2012) Kein schöner Land. Gesucht: Ein Schutzschirm gegen Risiken aus europäischen und deutschen Landinvestitionen in Entwicklungsländern. Stiftung Wissenschaft und Politik, Berlin. http://www.swp-berlin.org/fileadmin/contents/products/studien/2012_S19_rff.pdf

Rudolf B (ed) (2007), Menschenrecht Wasser? Peter Lang Verlag, Frankfurt a.M

Salman SMA, McInerney-Lankford S (2004) The Human Right to Water: Legal and Policy Dimensions. World Bank, Washington, D.C
Salomon ME (2013) Deprivation, Causation and the Law of International Cooperation. In: Langford M et al (eds) Global Justice, State Duties. The Extraterritorial Scope of Economic, Social, and Cultural Rights in International Law. Cambridge University Press, Cambridge, pp 259–296
Saul B et al (2014) The International Covenant on Economic, Social and Cultural Rights. Commentary, Cases and Materials. Oxford University Press, Oxford
Scheinin M (2001) The Right To Social Security. In: Eide A et al (eds) Economic, social and cultural rights. A textbook. 2nd edn. Nijhoff, Dordrecht, pp 211–222
Schieber GJ et al (2012) Health Financing in Ghana. World Bank, Washington, D.C
Schuering E, Gassmann F (2013) Whom to target—an obvious choice? In: Bender K et al (eds) Social Protection In Developing Countries. Reforming Systems. Routledge, Abingdon, pp 122–133
Scruggs L et al (2013Implementation of the Human Right to Social Security around the World. A Preliminary Analysis of National Social Protections Laws. In: Minkler L (ed) The State of Economic and Social Human Rights. A Global Overview. Cambridge University Press, Cambridge, pp 117–134
Ssenyonjo M (2009) Economic, Social and Cultural Rights in International Law. Hart, Oxford
Steiner Ch (2004) Das Recht auf soziale Gesundheitsversorgung. Lang, Frankfurt a.M
Stiglitz J (2004) Die Schatten der Globalisierung. Goldmann, Munich (original version 2002: globalization and its discontents. Norton, New York)
Sultana F (ed) (2012) The right to water. Politics, governance and social struggles. Earthscan, London
Surender R, Walker R (eds) (2013) Social policy in a developing world. Edward Elgar Publ, Cheltenham
Thielbörger P (2014) The right(s) to water. The multi-level governance of a unique human right. Springer, Berlin
Tobin J (2012) The right to health in International Law. Oxford University Press, Oxford
Tooze J (2007) The Rights to Social Security and Social Assistance: Towards an Analytical Framework. In: Baderin MA, McCorquodal R (eds) Economic, social and cultural rights in action. Oxford University Press, Oxford, pp 331–359
Townsend P (ed) (2009) Building Decent Societies. Rethinking the Role of Social Security in Development. Palgrave Macmillan, Basingstoke
United Nations (2013) The Millennium Development Goals Report 2013. United Nations, New York. http://www.un.org/millenniumgoals/pdf/report-2013/mdg-report-2013-english.pdf
United Nations (2014) The Millennium Development Goals Report 2014. United Nations, New York. http://www.un.org/millenniumgoals/2014%20MDG%20report/MDG%202014%20English%20web.pdf
van Langendonck J (ed) (2007) The right to social security. Intersentia, Antwerp
von Bernstorff J (2012) 'Land Grabbing' und Menschenrechte: Die FAO Voluntary Guidelines on the Responsible Governance of Tenure. INEF Forschungsreihe Menschenrechte, Unternehmensverantwortung und Nachhaltige Entwicklung 11/2012. http://www.humanrights-business.org/files/landgrabbing_final_1.pdf
WHO (2008) The world health report 2008. Primary health care: Now more than ever. WHO, Geneva. http://www.who.int/whr/2008/en/
WHO (2010) The world health report 2010. Health systems financing: the path to universal coverage. WHO, Geneva. http://www.who.int/whr/2010/en/
WHO/Providing for Health (P4H) initiative (2011) Ghana: coverage expansion through political commitment and innovative policy choices. Success Stories of Health Financing. Reforms for Universal Coverage. WHO, Geneva. http://www.who.int/providingforhealth/p4h_success_stories/en/index.html
Windfuhr M (2008) Armut, soziale Menschenrechte und das Recht auf soziale Sicherheit. Zeitschrift für Menschenrechte 2:81–99

Windfuhr M (2010) The World Food Crisis and the Right to Adequate Food. In: Gibney M, Skogly S (eds) Universal human rights and extraterritorial obligations. University of Pennsylvania Press, Philadelphia, pp 130–156

Winkler I T (2012) The human right to water. Significance, legal status and implications for water allocation. Hart, Oxford

Wolff J (2012) The human right to health. Norton, New York

World Bank (2012) Resilience, equity, and opportunity. The World Bank Social Protection and Labor Strategy 2012–22. World Bank, Washington, D.C. http://siteresources.worldbank.org/SOCIALPROTECTION/Resources/280558-1274453001167/7089867-1279223745454/7253917-1291314603217/SPL_Strategy_2012-22_FINAL.pdf

Ziegler J et al (2011) The fight for the right to food: lessons learned. Palgrave Macmillan, Basingstoke

Zuniga JM et al (eds) (2013) Advancing the Human Right to Health. Oxford University Press, Oxford

Documents of the Committee on Economic, Social and Cultural Rights (CESCR)

CESCR (1992) General Comment No. 4 on the right to adequate housing (Article11 [1]) of 1.1.1992, E/1992/23. http://www.refworld.org/docid/47a7079a1.html

CESCR (1999) General Comment No. 12 on the right to adequate food (Article 11) of 12.5.1999, E/C.12/1999/5. http://tbinternet.ohchr.org/_layouts/treatybodyexternal/Download.aspx?symbolno=E%2fC.12%2f1999%2f5&Lang=en

CESCR (2000) General Comment No. 14 on the right to the highest attainable standard of health (Article 12) of 11.8.2000, E/C.12/2000/4. http://tbinternet.ohchr.org/_layouts/treatybodyexternal/Download.aspx?symbolno=E%2fC.12%2f2000%2f4&Lang=en

CESCR (2003) General Comment No. 15 on the right to water (Arts. 11 and 12) of 20.1.2003, E/C.12/2002/11. http://tbinternet.ohchr.org/_layouts/treatybodyexternal/Download.aspx?symbolno=E%2fC.12%2f2002%2f11&Lang=en

CESCR (2008) General Comment No. 19 on the right to social security (Article 9) of 4.2.2008, E/C.12/GC/19. http://tbinternet.ohchr.org/_layouts/treatybodyexternal/Download.aspx?symbolno=E%2fC.12%2fGC%2f19&Lang=en

Chapter 5
Social Rights and the International Development Agenda

Abstract Human rights—and social rights in particular—are increasingly perceived as a central benchmark for the arrangement of objectives, policy programs and specific projects in international development policy. The debate on the integration of so-called rights-based approaches into multi- and bilateral development cooperation has contributed to the fact that politicians' acknowledgment of the relevance of social rights for development has risen considerably in recent years (Sect. 5.1). The *Social Protection Floors Initiative* of the ILO represents one example of a development agenda which is strictly oriented towards a rights-based approach (Sect. 5.2). Social human rights will also play a key role in the design of the *Post-2015 Development Agenda* which is currently being negotiated as a framework for the successor of the *Millennium Development Goals* (Sect. 5.3).

Keywords Rights-based approaches · Participation · Accountability · Social Protection Floors Initiative · Millennium Development Goals · Post-2015 Development Agenda

5.1 Social Rights-Based Approaches to Development

In the practice of development cooperation, linking poverty reduction programs with social rights is achieved mainly by so-called "Rights-based Approaches to Development".[1] In its policy paper of 2003, the *UN Development Group* (UNDG) summarized the central human rights principles which are to be followed by the different UN organizations when conceptualizing and implementing their

---

[1] Cf., inter alia, Gready and Ensor 2005; Hickey and Mitlin 2009; Sano 2007; Seppänen 2005; with a focus on the right to social security see Sepúlveda and Nyst 2012; Kaltenborn 2013; with regard to public health see Wilson 2009; Beracochea 2011. For detailed information on the rights based approach to development cooperation see also http://hrbaportal.org/. All websites cited in this chapter have been last accessed 3 September 2014.

M. Kaltenborn, *Social Rights and International Development*,
SpringerBriefs in Law, DOI 10.1007/978-3-662-45352-0_5

development aid programs.[2] Besides the principles of universality and inalienability, their indivisibility and inter-relatedness are highlighted above all. The realization of one right is indeed often dependent on the implementation of other rights: the right to health, for example, would not be protected in certain cases where there is no effective guarantee of the rights to education or to free access to information.[3] Equality and non-discrimination are additional principles that need to be considered as cross-organizational and cross-sectoral guidelines within the UN development cooperation framework.[4] Of special importance for a rights-based development policy are the principles of participation[5] and accountability[6]: they require that persons affected by development programs must be enabled to integrate their interests into the concrete decision making processes on the one hand, and, on the other, to claim their rights with independent supervisory authorities (e.g. national courts), or with quasi-judicial or informal and traditional review mechanisms. In this context, a rights-based approach also requires the financial and technical support of local civil society organizations.[7]

Not only the organizations assembled in the UNDG follow—at least in their official statements—the rights-based approach, but also numerous bilateral donors have made the commitment to human rights a central aspect of their development cooperation. In this regard, social rights are mostly considered to be explicitly included in the rights-based approach. This can be illustrated by using the example of the EU and the three largest—in terms of ODA volume—bilateral donor nations, the US, Great Britain and Germany.[8] The *USAID Strategy for Democracy, Human Rights and Governance* (DRG) published in 2003 states:

> USAID has a long history of supporting human rights under a variety of reporting labels, including rule of law, civil society, vulnerable populations, property rights and access to justice. This strategy makes human rights an explicit component of the Agency's approach to democratic development. It builds on USAID's existing portfolio of human rights programming, while elevating human rights, including economic, social and cultural rights, as a critical element of a development strategy that leverages the inclusion and dignity of all.[9] … The integration of DRG approaches across all development programs enables a greater focus on the promotion of individual and collective rights as a core objective of USAID's work. This focus can take many forms, from ensuring that humanitarian services are provided in a non-discriminatory manner that meets the distinct needs of all vulnerable groups, to promoting the provision of health services to vulnerable populations in a non-stigmatizing manner, to ensuring the equitable regulation of business, to mainstreaming the

---

[2] UNDG 2003.

[3] Ibid. p. 2.

[4] See Ratjen and Satija 2014; on a "right to social equality" see MacNaughton 2013.

[5] Hamm 2001, p. 1018; cf. also Dann 2012, pp. 255–258.

[6] Sano 2007, p. 72; see, generally, on the concept of "accountability" in development law Dann 2006.

[7] OCHCR, Frequently Asked Questions on a Human Rights-based Approach to Development Cooperation, 2006, p. 26, www.ohchr.org/Documents/Publications/FAQen.pdf.

[8] Cf. http://www.compareyourcountry.org/chart.php?project=oda&page=0&cr=oecd&lg=en.

[9] USAID 2013, p. 5.

protection of vulnerable groups into policy reform work. Activities to strengthen and reform institutions of economic governance can remove barriers to opportunity, for example, by strengthening property rights, reforming inheritance laws, and updating commercial law and improving its enforcement. Even some of the world's poorest can benefit from enhanced property rights that can unlock access to capital and wealth, and enable them to invest in their own prosperity. The leveraging of these rights-based approaches will enable the design and implementation of development programs that are better able to identify, affect and enfranchise marginalized groups, leading to more broad-based and sustainable development outcomes.[10]

The British government's development cooperation supports a number of civil society organizations via so-called *Programme Partnership Arrangements* (PPAs) with the main target of implementing, inter alia, social human rights, such as ActionAid, Avocats Sans Frontières (ASF), Care International UK, HelpAge International, OXFAM, or Save the Children.[11] The *Human Rights and Democracy Report 2013*, edited by the Foreign & Commonwealth Office (FCO), also highlights the link between human rights and development cooperation:

> The Department for International Development (DFID) … continued its work to support the human rights of poor and marginalised people in developing countries with the objective of ensuring that everybody can enjoy the economic, social, civil, political and cultural rights defined in internationally agreed human rights treaties.[12] The realisation of all human rights underpins sustainable development. Through its development programmes, the UK supports civil society and governments to build open economies and open societies in which citizens have freedom, dignity, choice and control over their lives. UK Aid also works to ensure that all segments of society, including the persistently poor, women, ethnic minorities and other marginalised groups, can gainfully participate in growth processes by tackling the specific barriers they face in accessing economic opportunities.[13]

The German federal government comments on the importance of social rights for its cooperation with developing countries in a similar manner:

> The Human rights-based approach puts the focus on the structural causes of poverty and social exclusion. It helps to make power relations within society more equitable, and contributes to sustainable poverty reduction.[14] The realisation of civil, political, economic, social and cultural rights is the key to successful poverty reduction—for poverty can be understood as a denial of human rights; in effect, it means exclusion from access to basic resources and social services such as water and sanitation, health care, energy services, primary education, justice and political participation.[15]

Finally in this context, the EU's efforts of attaching greater value to the promotion of social rights in its development policy are of note. Although the *European Instrument for Democracy and Human Rights (EIDHR) Strategy Paper*

---

[10] USAID 2013, p. 26.

[11] https://www.gov.uk/programme-partnership-arrangements-ppas.

[12] FCO 2013, p. 21.

[13] Ibid. p. 28.

[14] BMZ 2011, p. 7.

[15] Ibid. p. 11.

2011–2013 focuses on political rights and fundamental freedoms,[16] it is also recognized that social rights need to be attributed greater attention in European foreign policy:

> (T)here is an increasingly consensual understanding that the fulfilment of the international human rights agenda also requires increased efforts to protect and promote economic, social and cultural rights.[17] EIDHR's aim is to finance activities to enhance human dignity worldwide, through the protection and promotion of ALL human rights, including the ratification of relevant international conventions and protocols. Moreover, the EIDHR will strengthen its role in supporting initiatives to protect and promote economic, social and cultural rights, including by advocating for the signature and ratification/accession of the CESCR and of its optional protocol.[18]

Likewise, some of the numerous public-private partnerships engaging globally, particularly in the area of health and food security, refer to social human rights in their policy papers. As an example, the *Global Fund to Fight AIDS, Tuberculosis and Malaria* is mentioned here, that commits explicitly to a rights-based approach:

> A human rights-based approach to health and to addressing HIV, TB and malaria, means integrating human rights norms and principles in the design, implementation, monitoring, and evaluation of disease programs. These principles include human dignity, non-discrimination, transparency, and accountability. A human rights-based approach also means empowering vulnerable groups and key populations, ensuring their participation in decision-making processes which concern them, as well as incorporating accountability mechanisms which they can access.[19]

Even though great attention is meanwhile given to social human rights in the framework of global and bilateral development cooperation, the rights-based approach does not play a big role in other areas of development policy yet. This approach is given only a cursory reference in the discussion on aid effectiveness, which is nowadays one of the most important and most influential debates on development cooperation.[20] The *Doha Development Agenda* of the WTO, again one of the main documents of contemporary development policy, even refrains entirely from making a direct reference to social rights, although close links between international trade law and the protection of human rights are evident.[21] The third major regulatory complex of global development policy—the resolutions and declarations adopted by the UN on the occasion of the turn of the millennium—includes the basic commitment to "all internationally recognized human rights and

---

[16] Cf. inter alia European Commission 2010, Paras 39, 57.

[17] Ibid. Para 9.

[18] Ibid. Para 33; cf. in this context also OECD/DAC 2007, as well as in detail on rights-based approaches in development policy of individual donor countries World Bank and OECD 2013, pp. 141–243.

[19] Global Fund 2014, p. 5; see also Global Fund 2011, Paras 70–75; cf. Davis 2014.

[20] *Accra Agenda for Action*, 2008, http://www.oecd.org/dac/effectiveness/34428351.pdf, Para 3, 13c; *The Busan Partnership for Effective Development Co-operation*, 2011, http://www.oecd.org/dac/effectiveness/49650173.pdf, Para 22.

[21] See supra 3.4.

fundamental freedoms, including the right to development"[22]; the MDGs however, particularly important to development policy practice, reflect only to a limited degree the rights-based approach.[23] In this context, the legendary metaphor of "ships passing in the night" used by Philip Alston to illustrate the relationship between human rights and development policy,[24] has preserved parts of its validity until today. During the *Fourth High Level Forum on Aid Effectiveness* in Busan in 2011, the participants of the *Thematic Session on Rights-Based Approaches to Development* came to the right conclusion that

> (i)t is time to break the divide between human rights, aid, and economic policies. Human rights and the rights-based approach should be shared values and principles for all development stakeholders.[25]

The negotiations on the *Post-2015 Development Agenda*, that are, according to the report of the *High-level Panel of Eminent Persons*, committed to the goal of "Leave no one behind",[26] offer the chance to eventually and comprehensively unite human rights and development policy. Due to persisting controversies on connecting lines of both policy fields,[27] and especially against the background of a changed donor landscape,[28] however, it will be not an easy task at all.

5.2 Basic Social Rights for All: The ILO Social Protection Floor and the Global Fund for Social Protection

The so-called *Social Protection Floor* (*SPF*) *Initiative* has been mentioned several times in this study. Among many projects on poverty reduction initiated by various stages of global social policy, it stands out in so far that it focuses explicitly on the functions of law—in particular of constitutional law and social welfare law—in implementing global poverty reduction strategies[29]: During the 101st Session of the *International Labour Conference* in July 2012, the *Social Protection Floors* (*SPF*)

---

[22] *United Nations Millennium Declaration*, UN-Doc. A/RES/55/2, 18.9.2000, http://www.un.org/millennium/declaration/ares552e.htm, Para 24.

[23] See infra Sect. 4.3

[24] See supra Chap. 1 footnote 4.

[25] Full Busan Proceedings—including all session summaries and speeches, http://www.oecd.org/dac/effectiveness/Final%20file.pdf, p. 108.

[26] Alston 2005.

[27] Cf., for example, on the question, whether ODA performance obligations can be based on human rights, supra Sect. 3.3.

[28] See http://www.oecd.org/dac/dac-global-relations/non-dac-reporting.htm.

[29] See the detailed analysis of the legal framework of social protection systems in ILO 2011; generally on the initiative see Cichon et al. 2011; Liebert 2011; Deacon 2013a.

Recommendation[30] was adopted. This requests the Member States to introduce basic protection schemes providing for access to primary health care and a minimum of income security for all inhabitants, and also to raise this basic protection scheme continuously up to the level of existing ILO agreements.[31] Both aspects are rightly considered to be important because the introduction of basic protection must not be misused as a pretext for not undertaking additional efforts in favor of a country's own population.[32] The form of social protection, such as social assistance programs, social insurance, etc. is to be chosen by the countries and remains within the ambit of their own socio-political strategy.[33] The basis for the new *soft law* instrument is the *SPF Initiative*, which was initiated in 2009 by the UN as an international alliance, mainly supported by the ILO and its sister agency, the WHO, but also integrating many other UN bodies and development cooperation partners. It remains to be seen whether the necessary implementation measures on the ground will follow the international appeal to the community of States. Currently, the *SPF Initiative* assists many countries in the process of deciding whether such basic systems can be fully or partially implemented on the national level.[34]

From a legal point of view, the fact that the *SPF Recommendation* formulates several basic principles which have gained consensus among the international community and which might potentially be of relevance for further development of other social rights, is considered important. According to Para 3 of the Recommendation, ILO Member States have to respect the following principles when establishing social security systems:

---

[30] *Recommendation concerning National Floors of Social Protection (SPF Recommendation)*, Recommendation 102, http://www.ilo.org/dyn/normlex/en/f?p=NORMLEXPUB:12100:0::NO:12100:P12100_INSTRUMENT_ID:3065524:NO. See, generally, on the relationship between the SPF Recommendation and the ICESCR, Mestrum 2014; Cichon 2014.

[31] Para 13 *SPF Recommendation*.

[32] This is in fact a critical point because—as Deacon 2013b, p. 228, rightly points out—"the history of welfare states developed in the twentieth century, social policy and social development science tells us that the better way to reduce poverty is fairly consistent and involves middle-class buy-into inclusive state welfare provision. … (T)he political economy of welfare-state building … teaches us that this requires the construction of cross-alliances and middle-class buy-in to reform."; (cf. also Deacon 2013a, pp. 159–160). This problem, however, has of course been realized by the advocates of the *Social Protection Floor*. As Cichon et al. 2011, p. 9, emphasize, it is "critical to ensure that public social security systems include and are supported by all strata of the population, including the rich and the better off, in order to maintain and strengthen broad public support and national solidarity. Such a broad national consensus will protect the necessary fiscal space and maintain pressure to assure the quality of provision. A broad national consensus can best be maintained by ensuring that all people perceive the potential benefits as worthwhile pillars of their risk management strategies. Solidarity works best when providing benefits for all. As the famous health economist Brian Abel-Smith once said: A system for the poor alone will always be a poor system".

[33] Para 9 *SPF Recommendation*.

[34] For more information on social protection floors see http://www.socialprotectionfloor-gateway.org/index.html; cf. also ILO 2014, pp. 145–159.

(a) the universality of protection, based on social solidarity; (b) entitlement to benefits prescribed by national law; (c) adequacy and predictability of benefits; (d) non-discrimination, gender equality and responsiveness to special needs; (e) social inclusion, including of persons in the informal economy; (f) respect for the rights and dignity of people covered by the social security guarantees; (g) progressive realization, including by setting targets and time frames; (h) solidarity in financing while seeking to achieve an optimal balance between the responsibilities and interests among those who finance and benefit from social security schemes; (i) consideration of diversity of methods and approaches, including of financing mechanisms and delivery systems; (j) transparent, accountable and sound financial management and administration; (k) financial, fiscal and economic sustainability with due regard to social justice and equity; (l) coherence with social, economic and employment policies; (m) coherence across institutions responsible for delivery of social protection; (n) high-quality public services that enhance the delivery of social security systems; (o) efficiency and accessibility of complaint and appeal procedures; (p) regular monitoring of implementation, and periodic evaluation; (q) full respect for collective bargaining and freedom of association for all workers; and (r) tripartite participation with representative organizations of employers and workers, as well as consultation with other organizations of persons concerned.

Besides the financing of basic social protection systems, the implementation of these principles will probably be the biggest challenge for governments.[35] The special importance of the exchange of information and experience among developing countries, as well as the technical support of the industrialized countries and the ILO, is separately highlighted in Para 24 of the Recommendation.

Another aspect is particularly noteworthy from a legal perspective: Although the ILO is not the only international organization which has recently dedicated special attention to social security—the subject has also been upgraded considerably in the development policy work of UNICEF,[36] the FAO,[37] the *World Bank*[38] and the EU[39]—it is striking indeed that the ILO pursues, in a considerably stronger way than the other international actors, an approach which is consistently rights-based.[40] Social security should be based on statutory, clearly defined en-titlements that can

---

[35] See also Walker 2013, p. 282.

[36] UNICEF 2012.

[37] HLPE 2012.

[38] See recently World Bank 2012; cf. also Vetterlein 2007; on the question to what extent *Poverty Reduction Strategy Papers* (PRSPs), which have been used by the *World Bank* as planning tool, can have an impact on poverty reduction indeed, see Siebold 2008.

[39] Communication of the EU-Commission on Social Protection in European Union Development Cooperation, 20.8.2012, COM(2012) 446 final.

[40] Furthermore, the rights-based approach is especially highlighted in the UNICEF report, UNICEF 2012, p. 49. On the role of civil society in enforcing the right to social security, see also Communication of the EU-Commission on Social Protection in European Union Development Cooperation, 20.8.2012, COM(2012) 446 final, p. 9: "Civil society and the social partners should be empowered and encouraged to partner with the state in developing and implementing social protection systems. Their participation can help promote efficiency in provision as well as wider consultation and inclusion. They can play a key role as advocates for social protection as well as empowering communities and individuals, in particular the disadvantaged and excluded, through raising awareness and improving information. In some instances, they can also help in monitoring and evaluating social protection schemes."

be claimed by citizens at institutions in charge.[41] Of special importance are, furthermore, the participation rights of those among the population who easily run the risk, especially with regard to projects requiring a higher degree of bureaucratic effort, of not always being sufficiently respected.

In contrast to other social rights, the right to social security generally requires the development of larger and long-lasting organizational structures[42]: Old age and health insurance schemes, as well as country-wide social assistance programs, call for a comparably high degree of institutionalization and need adequately trained staff for their administration. However, this complexity, significant for institutions of social protection, should not be held as an excuse to deprive affected citizens of their right to participation. On the contrary, a rights-based approach implies the guarantee of a high degree of participation on all national levels of implementation relevant for the right to social security—from the legislative process to the concrete program design (which is generally done at the ministerial level), up to the on-site application to the individual case. It is, therefore, necessary to have in place, from a legal perspective, sufficiently structured access to information and participation. These structures should be open to interested civil society actors, such as political parties, trade unions and NGOs, as well as to citizens concerned with the handling of their individual case.

The social protection standards of the ILO already accommodate this central element of the rights-based approach: Participation is one of the main principles of the *Social Security (Minimum Standards) Convention* which can be regarded as ILO's primary document on social protection.[43] But also the *SPF Recommendation* requires—as already mentioned above—the safeguarding of the "tripartite participation with representative organizations of employers and workers, as well as consultation with other relevant and representative organizations of persons concerned"[44] during all planning stages of social protection systems. The principlè of participation does not entail an automatic preference for certain organizational structures in the field of social protection. A system of social self-administration, such as the German system, in which public authorities only have supervisory roles to ensure the conformity with the legal framework, while all relevant decisions on implementation are taken by the actors and representatives of self-governing bodies themselves, may be well-suited to serve this principle in daily practice. However, State-based organizational structures that refrain from delegating tasks to non-governmental self-governing bodies can likewise be designed in a "participation-friendly" way.

---

41 Para 3(b), 7 *SPF Recommendation*.

42 The following three paragraphs have already been published in Kaltenborn 2013, pp. 58–59; cf. also Sepúlveda and Nyst 2012, pp. 54, 58, 60, 62.

43 Cf. Articles 6, 72 ILO Convention No. 102 (see supra 4.3); for other principles of this Convention see Kulke/Cichon/Pal 2007:16).

44 See Para 3.r, 8(d) *SPF Recommendation*.

From a human rights perspective, the principle of accountability is equally important for the implementation of the right to social security: In order to detect and remove inadequate or defective implementation of social protection schemes, monitoring mechanisms that are transparent to civil society need to be established.[45] Moreover, there need to be clear rules and functioning institutions that enable individuals to claim their rights. It is noteworthy that this does not only apply to the substantive entitlements in the respective social protection programs, but also to participation and other procedural rights—an issue which is often overlooked. Already *ILO Convention No. 102* requires its Member States to integrate efficient monitoring and complaint procedures into their social protection systems.[46] The recent *SPF Recommendation* provides a more concise understanding of the qualitative requirements which must be fulfilled by these procedures:

> Basic social security guarantees should be established by law. National laws and regulations should specify the range, qualifying conditions and levels of the benefits giving effect to these guarantees. Impartial, transparent, effective, simple, rapid, accessible and inexpensive complaint and appeal procedures should also be specified. Access to complaint and appeal procedures should be free of charge to the applicant. Systems should be in place that enhance compliance with national legal frameworks.[47]

The *SPF Recommendation* is no legally binding instrument of international law. However, due to its *soft law* character, the document provides an important orientation, both for drawing up new social protection systems and for reforming existing systems. In political discussions, actors involved in the legislative process may use it as a reference to accommodate—on the basis of a rights-based approach—the principles of participation and accountability in the design of health care systems, old age protection schemes and basic social protection programs.

Based on the *SPF Initiative*, the former *UN Special Rapporteurs on the Right to Food* and *on Extreme Poverty and Human Rights*, Olivier De Schutter and Magdalena Sepulveda, have, furthermore, developed a proposal to establish a *Global Fund for Social Protection*.[48] Essentially, it will consist of two components: On the one hand, a facility branch should be established in order to close funding shortfalls faced especially by the least developed countries (LDCs) when setting up their social protection floors.[49] On the other hand, it is also necessary to safeguard those situations via a reinsurance branch where developing countries are struck by unexpected bigger crises—for example, natural disasters, the sudden breakdown of export markets or global economic and financial crises. In such extraordinary periods, social security systems are often used to such an extent, that system breakdown is possible in most extreme cases. When social security is implemented

---

[45] See Para 19 *SPF Recommendation*.

[46] Article 70 *ILO Convention No. 102*.

[47] Para 7 *SPF Recommendation*.

[48] De Schutter and Sepúlveda 2012; see also Deacon 2013a, pp. 173–178.

[49] See, generally, on the issue of financing national social protection floors Cichon et al. 2011, pp. 9–10.

using a rights-based approach,[50] crisis situations have an even more tremendous effect, as governments are confronted with enforceable, if applicable, legal claims by members of society. This also happens in times when the national budget is already encumbered by other mandatory crisis management operations. Reinsurance via a *Global Fund* would considerably encourage developing countries to introduce national social protection floors. The financing of the fund would be borne by both poorer and richer members of the international community, so that eventually both sides, as de Schutter and Sepúlveda rightly point out, could comply with their social rights obligations:

> The Global Fund for Social Protection could provide the vital support needed by States in order to make social protection for all a reality. The concept for the GFSP relies on commitments made by all States that stem from their human rights obligations. It relies on poorer States, or LDCs, devoting their maximum available resources to domestic social protection systems grounded in human rights in an effort to provide at least the basic social protection floor. It then relies on the richer countries, those in a position to assist and which have a duty of international assistance and cooperation, to help meet the gap between what poorer States are able to provide and the social protection floor. Establishing the GFSP would provide a means for both sets of commitments to work in tandem.[51] The GFSP should be designed to ensure that LDCs make commitments to adopt or expand human rights based social protection systems, and that developed countries provide financial support. … The GFSP would ensure a long-term perspective and predictability in providing assistance as well as coordination amongst the international donor community, necessary for the effectiveness and sustainability of social protection, and would avoid a short-sighted, uncoordinated and fragmented approach from donors.[52]

Of course, several questions concerning the specific design of such a *Global Fund* still remain open: Various alternatives for the technical implementation of a reinsurance branch are possible,[53] moreover the institutional form, the concrete volume of the fund and, last but not least, the allocation of shares to be borne by individual States and groups of States, respectively, also need to be elaborated in more detail. The ratio of donor States' shares, in particular is, as we have seen already, not unambiguously determined in international law: The fact that industrialized nations are legally bound to aid is unarguable; the exact extent of this assistance is, however, not clearly defined by human rights law.[54] Also, relevant *soft law*, such as, for example, the 0.7 % rule, which was repeatedly confirmed in the past, only provides vague indications in this regard, as the activities to be financed via the *Global Fund* will be obviously a mere sub-aspect of the broad spectrum of global cooperation, despite the fact that they especially serve the main development policy objective of sustainable poverty reduction. The *SPF Recommendation* was also formulated reticently in this regard:

---

[50] See supra 5.1.

[51] De Schutter and Sepúlveda 2012, pp. 10–11.

[52] De Schutter and Sepúlveda 2012, p. 20.

[53] In more detail De Schutter and Sepúlveda 2012, pp. 15–19.

[54] See supra 3.3.

> National social protection floors should be financed by national resources. Members whose economic and fiscal capacities are insufficient to implement the guarantees may seek international cooperation and support that complement their own efforts.[55]

This special emphasis on the financial efforts to be made by developing countries themselves might be welcomed, given the reduction of dependencies on external aid payments that it entails. On the other hand, such a reluctance towards extra-territorial obligations can also be seen from a critical point of view.[56] Hence, many indications support the approach of making use of the *Post-2015 Agenda* negotiations, not only to pursue the *Social Protection Floor-Initiative*, but also to put the idea of the *Global Fund for Social Protection* into more concrete terms and thereby negotiate the precise amounts of holding, particularly on the side of donor States. For a fairly long period of time, such a *Global Fund* would enable the safeguarding of national efforts to establish social protection floors, which, although not necessarily legally actionable, would at least be politically reliable.

5.3 Millennium Development Goals and the United Nations Post-2015 Development Agenda

The *Millennium Development Goals* (MDGs), announced in 2000 by the UN, are without any doubt the best known and the most important global initiative on poverty reduction in recent years.[57] Chapter 4 has already discussed its impact on the implementation of individual social rights—in particular, the rights to food, to access to clean drinking water, to adequate housing, and to health. Even though the MDGs themselves do not refer explicitly to the respective rights,[58] at least the *UN Millennium Declaration*, the unanimously adopted legal document upon which the MDGs are based, underlines the obligation of UN Member States "(t)o respect fully and uphold the Universal Declaration of Human Rights" and "(t)o strive for the full protection and promotion … of civil, political, economic, social and cultural rights for all".[59] In particular, the main development policy goal, the fight against extreme poverty, is directly linked with the realization of a number of social rights. Programs on the fight against poverty help to ameliorate food supply, improve public health and housing, lead to the improvement of educational opportunities, and

---

[55] Para 12 *SPF Recommendation.*

[56] See Deacon 2013a, p. 158: "(T)he watering down of the reference to international financial support to that being possibly necessary only initially and only in the poorest countries, flowing as it does with the fashion to stress to emphasise on national fiscal responsibility, undermines the case of those who still call for global taxes for global public goods".

[57] http://www.undp.org/content/undp/en/home/mdgoverview/.

[58] See Karimova 2014, p. 183.

[59] UN Doc. A/55/L.2, 18.9.2000, http://www.un.org/millennium/declaration/ares552e.pdf, Para 25; for the Follow-up to the outcome of the Millennium Summit see http://unstats.un.org/unsd/mdg/Host.aspx?Content=/Products/GAResolutions.htm.

contribute to reducing discrimination against certain groups of population. The close connection that exists between social human rights and the fight against extreme poverty has also been highlighted by the *Human Rights Council*. Based on a report presented by the former *Special Rapporteur on Extreme Poverty and Human Rights*, Magdalena Sepulveda, the Council adopted the *Guiding Principles on Extreme Poverty and Human Rights*[60] in September 2012, which state, inter alia:

> Poverty is an urgent human rights concern in itself. It is both a cause and a consequence of human rights violations and an enabling condition for other violations. Not only is extreme poverty characterized by multiple reinforcing violations of civil, political, economic, social and cultural rights, but persons living in poverty generally experience regular denials of their dignity and equality.[61] … Persons living in poverty are confronted by the most severe obstacles—physical, economic, cultural and social—to accessing their rights and entitlements. Consequently, they experience many interrelated and mutually reinforcing deprivations—including dangerous work conditions, unsafe housing, lack of nutritious food, unequal access to justice, lack of political power and limited access to health care—that prevent them from realizing their rights and perpetuate their poverty. Persons experiencing extreme poverty live in a vicious cycle of powerlessness, stigmatization, discrimination, exclusion and material deprivation, which all mutually reinforce one another.[62] … Extreme poverty is a clear illustration of the indivisibility, interrelatedness and interdependence of human rights, given that persons living in poverty face daily violations of their civil, cultural, economic, political and social rights, which interact and mutually reinforce one another with devastating effects.[63]

As an interim assessment of MDG 1, one can conclude that during recent years, considerable success could have been achieved in this area: Target 1.A, stating that the proportion of those people that have an income of less than 1.25 USD per day should be halved between 1990 and 2015, has since been reached, according to *World Bank* estimations.[64] Although approximately 1.2 billion people were still living in extreme poverty in 2010, these are 700 million fewer than in 1990. It is assumed that in 2015, approximately 970 million people in low or middle income countries will still suffer from extreme poverty. Sub-Saharan Africa and South Asia will probably be home to 40 per cent each of all those living in extreme poverty in developing countries. However, not only the poorest States face this difficulty;

---

[60] UN Doc. A/HRC/21/11, 28.10.2012, http://daccess-dds-ny.un.org/doc/RESOLUTION/GEN/G12/176/77/PDF/G1217677.pdf?OpenElement. The *UN General Assembly* has denominated the *Guiding Principles* as a "useful tool for States in the formulation and implementation of poverty reduction and eradication policies, as appropriate" and has required all governmental and non-governmental actors "to consider the guiding principles in the formulation and implementation of their policies and measures concerning persons affected by extreme poverty", UN Doc. A/RES/67/164, 20.12.2012, http://www.un.org/en/ga/search/view_doc.asp?symbol=A/RES/67/164.

[61] Final draft of the guiding principles on extreme poverty and human rights, submitted by the Special Rapporteur on extreme poverty and human rights, Magdalena Sepúlveda Carmona, UN Doc. A/HRC/21/39, 18.7.2012, http://daccess-dds-ny.un.org/doc/UNDOC/GEN/G12/154/60/PDF/G1215460.pdf?OpenElement, Para 3.

[62] Ibid. Para 4.

[63] Ibid. Para 16.

[64] On the following see United Nations 2014, pp. 6–7.

many transition countries have also not yet managed—despite some remarkable progress[65]—to create basic conditions for all parts of the population allowing for a life above the poverty line.[66]

Not only in the field of fight against poverty, but also generally, it seems history will view the MDGs, at least primarily, as a successful project.[67] However, it should not be overlooked that the concept and implementation of this initiative has been seriously criticized.[68] Most likely, we can refute the argument that the MDGs are deficient and constituted an incomplete development agenda due to the absence of essential development core challenges such as peacekeeping and the promotion of democracy and good governance structures within their provisions.[69] These aspects are not only mentioned in the *Millennium Declaration*, but also in a variety of other basic global documents. It can be debated, of course, whether proper priority-setting is achieved by the selection of the MDGs; it would not be fair to say, however, that all other objectives which have been quite rightly incorporated in international treaties or in other global *soft law* documents have receded entirely into the background. Other objections seem to be more serious. The fact that the MDGs are primarily formulated as quantitative targets leads to the concealment of persisting or even growing inequalities within the respective countries. Furthermore, discrimination against certain demographic groups is a problem, as is the fact that certain widely important qualitative issues are left out of account, in particular in areas such as education, food, health. Furthermore, the structural causes of poverty (especially the unequal distribution of land and capital within a society) are not sufficiently addressed. The relation of global targets and national implementation has not always succeeded, as States are confronted in differing degrees with the issues mentioned in the MDGs. And, finally, it has often been claimed that the drafting process was deficient, as a small group of donor States was substantially involved in the formulation of the MDG catalogue, whereas the influence of governments of the global South was rather low. As a consequence thereof, the formulation of MDG 8 was, without doubt, rightly criticized. It contained the requirement "to create a global partnership for development", focusing on the responsibility of rich members

---

65 For example in China the proportion of people living on less than 1,25 USD fell from 60 per cent in 1990 to 12 per cent in 2010; United Nations 2014, p. 7.

66 UNDP 2013.

67 Cf. the foreword of UN General Secretary *Ban Ki-Moon* to the MDG report 2014 (United Nations 2014, p. 3): "The Millennium Development Goals (MDGs) have been the most successful global anti-poverty push in history. Significant and substantial progress has been made in meeting many of the targets—including halving the number of people living in extreme poverty and the proportion of people without sustainable access to improved sources of drinking water. The proportion of urban slum dwellers declined significantly. Remarkable gains have been made in the fight against malaria and tuberculosis. There have been visible improvements in all health areas as well as primary education. …".

68 Cf. Manning 2009, pp. 42–59; Loewe 2010, pp. 110–117; see also European Union 2013, pp. 21–22.

69 Holtz 2010, p. 7.

of the international community, but not containing any specific, quantifiable obligations of industrialized States.

From a human rights perspective, one central point of critique is to be highlighted: Even in the (unlikely) case that all MDG targets will be achieved, only a part of the human population could actually enjoy the social rights corresponding with the respective MDGs.[70] Or, to put it differently: According to the approach of the MDGs, it has been taken into account *ex ante* that in the case of the successful meeting of targets, basic social human rights are still being infringed on countless occasions. In this regard, MDG 1 is the most distinctive example: The target is considered to be reached, even though more than one billion people still live in extreme poverty! This might be justified as a reality-based, pragmatic approach to handle global poverty issues; critics, however, would denounce this point of view, not without good reason, as cynicism. At any rate, this point of critique was addressed during the negotiations on the *Post-2015 Development Agenda*.[71] The report of the *High-Level Panel of Eminent Persons on the Post-2015 Development Agenda* (HLP) highlights the requirement "Leave no one behind" as one of the core subjects for the formulation of new development targets:

> The next development agenda must ensure that in the future neither income nor gender, nor ethnicity, nor disability, nor geography, will determine whether people live or die, whether a mother can give birth safely, or whether her child has a fair chance in life. We must keep faith with the promise of the MDGs and now finish the job. The MDGs aspired to halve poverty. After 2015 we should aspire to put an end to hunger and extreme poverty as well as addressing poverty in all its other forms. This is a major new commitment to everyone on the planet who feels marginalised or excluded, and to the neediest and most vulnerable people, to make sure their concerns are addressed and that they can enjoy their human rights. The new agenda must tackle the causes of poverty, exclusion and inequality. … These are issues of basic social justice. Many people living in poverty have not had a fair chance in life because they are victims of illness or poor healthcare, unemployment, a natural disaster, climate change, local conflict, instability, poor local leadership, or low-quality education—or have been given no schooling at all. Others face discrimination. Remedying these fundamental inequalities and injustices is a matter of respect for people's universal human rights. A focus on the poorest and most marginalised, a disproportionate number of whom are women, follows directly from the principles agreed to in the Millennium Declaration and at Rio. These principles should remain the foundation of the post-2015 agenda.[72]

In July 2014, the *UN General Assembly's Open Working Group on Sustainable Development Goals* forwarded to the GA its proposal for a set of the new development goals and targets.[73] The proposal refers to the outcome document of the *UN*

---

[70] On that and on further points of critique cf. Alston 2005, p. 762 et seqq; Schmidt-Traub 2009, pp. 77–78; Engelhardt 2010, pp. 1135–1136. See, for a detailed discussion of the relationship between human rights and the MDGs, Nelson 2007, and the articles in Langford et al. 2013.

[71] For an overview of the current state of negotiations see http://www.undp.org/content/undp/en/home/mdgoverview/mdg_goals/post-2015-development-agenda/. See, generally, on the new agenda Melamed 2012; Kaul 2013; Beisheim 2012; Loewe 2012 and 2014; Janus and Keijzer 2013; Alonso et al. 2013; Higgins 2013; Global Policy Forum Europe and terre des hommes 2013.

[72] HLP 2013, p. 7.

[73] http://sustainabledevelopment.un.org/focussdgs.html.

Conference on Sustainable Development in Rio de Janeiro 2012, which explicitly underlined the importance of respect for all human rights,[74] and turns the focus to several global issues which are closely connected to essential social rights.[75] It is to be hoped that these ambitious objectives can be maintained in the final stages of the Post 2015 negotiations.

The orientation towards a rights-based approach should be at the center of the new development agenda.[76] Social rights will play a key role in this context. If the ultimate ambition of the international community is indeed, corresponding to the recommendations of the HLP report, the complete eradication of extreme poverty in the world, this would mandatorily imply the rigorous implementation of at least the core obligations arising from the social rights embedded in the UDHR and in the ICESCR—namely, both from the right to adequate living standard and the right to health and particularly from the right to social security, which has not been granted sufficient significance, at least not during the initial period of MDG implementation.[77] The extraterritorial obligations of industrialized nations arising from their

---

[74] UN Doc. A/RES/66/288, 27.7.2012, http://daccess-dds-ny.un.org/doc/UNDOC/GEN/N11/476/10/PDF/N1147610.pdf?OpenElement.

[75] Particularly noteworthy from a social rights perspective are Goal 1 (End poverty in all its forms everywhere, inter alia [target 1.3] implement nationally appropriate social protection systems and measures for all, including floors, and by 2030 achieve substantial coverage of the poor and the vulnerable), Goal 2 (End hunger, achieve food security and improved nutrition, and promote sustainable agriculture), Goal 3 (Ensure healthy lives and promote well-being for all at all ages, inter alia [target 3.8] achieve universal health coverage (UHC), including financial risk protection, access to quality essential health care services), Goal 6 (Ensure availability and sustainable management of water and sanitation for all), Goal 10 (Reduce inequality within and among countries; inter alia [target 10.2] empower and promote the social, economic and political inclusion of all irrespective of age, sex, disability, race, ethnicity, origin, religion or economic or other status) and Goal 11 (Make cities and human settlements inclusive, safe, resilient and sustainable, inter alia [target 11.1] ensure access for all to adequate, safe and affordable housing and basic services, and upgrade slums).

[76] Cf. UNHCHR 2013; Marks 2014; Human Rights for All Post-2015: A Litmus Test, June 2014, http://www.cesr.org/downloads/HRs.Post2015.litmus.test.pdf; see also the Submission by the *UN Special Rapporteur on extreme poverty and human rights* on "The Post-2015 Development Agenda: Prioritising people living in poverty through goals on inequalities, social protection and access to justice", http://www.ohchr.org/Documents/Issues/EPoverty/Post205SubmissionSR23April2013.pdf: "(I)t is first and foremost crucial that the post-2015 development agenda is underpinned by and premised on human rights. Human rights standards and principles provide concrete guidance as to how goals and targets should be framed. Governments have already committed to uphold human rights in numerous international treaties; however these existing legal obligations and norms have been largely overlooked in current development policy".

[77] The UN Special Procedures mandate-holders have rightly claimed in a joint statement published in May 2013 that "(t)he post-2015 agenda should include a goal on the provision of social protection floors, explicitly referencing the right to social security and a human rights-based approach to social protection". Moreover, they have formulated two additional recommendations concerning key priorities for the Post-2015 development agenda: "The post-2015 agenda should incorporate equality as a stand-alone and cross-cutting goal, aiming to progressively eliminate disparities within and between the most marginalized groups and the general population as well as between countries in order to achieve more inclusive forms of development." … "Accountability

human rights obligations[78] provide the legal basis for international cooperation in the framework of the *Post-2015 Agenda*: They make clear that the global fight against poverty is a task that does not concern solely countries of the global South, but constitutes an international legal obligation of the entire international community.

References

Alonso JA et al (eds) (2013) Alternative development strategies in the post-2015 era. Bloomsbury, London

Alston Ph (2005) Ships Passing in the Night. The Current State of the Human Rights and Development Debate seen through the lens of the Millennium Development Goals. HRQ 25:755–829

Beisheim M (2012) Post-2015 Sustainable Development Goals. UN Negotiations Begin. SWP Comments. http://www.swp-berlin.org/fileadmin/contents/products/comments/2012C36_bsh.pdf

Beracochea E (ed) (2011) Rights-based approaches to public health. Springer, New York

BMZ (2011) Human Rights in German Development Policy, BMZ Strategy Paper 4, BMZ, Bonn. http://www.bmz.de/en/publications/type_of_publication/strategies/Strategiepapier305_04_2011.pdf

Cichon M (2014) ILO Recommendation 202 is Not a Legal Island: Explicit Links between R. 202, the ICESCR and the UDHR, in: UNRISD resource platform for practitioners and policy makers Linking Social Protection and Human Rights. http://www.unrisd.org/UNRISD/website/newsview.nsf/(httpNews)/CBBBE10B1A747BD2C1257CCA004BC23D?OpenDocument

Cichon M et al (2011) The UN Social Protection Floor Initiative: Turning the Tide at the ILO Conference 2011, Friedrich-Ebert-Stiftung, International Policy Analysis 2011. http://library.fes.de/pdf-files/iez/07814.pdf

Dann Ph (2006) Accountability in Development Aid Law: The World Bank, UNDP and Emerging Structures of Transnational Oversight. AVR 44:381–404

Dann Ph (2012) Entwicklungsverwaltungsrecht. Theorie und Dogmatik des Rechts der Entwicklungszusammenarbeit, untersucht am Beispiel der Weltbank, der EU und der Bundesrepublik Deutschland. Mohr Siebeck, Tübingen (English version 2013: The Law of Development Cooperation. A comparative analysis of the World Bank, the EU and Germany. Cambridge University Press, Cambridge)

Davis SLM (2014) Human Rights and the Global Fund to Fight AIDS, Tuberculosis, and Malaria. Health Hum Rights J 16:134–147

Deacon B (2013a) Global Social Policy in the Making. Policy Press, Bristol

Deacon B (2013b) Globalization and social policy in developing countries. In: Surender R, Walker R (eds) Social policy in a developing world. Edward Elgar Publishing, Cheltenham, pp 217–236

(Footnote 77 continued)
must be at the core of the post-2015 development framework. We propose the establishment of a double accountability mechanism, whereby accountability mechanisms are developed at both national and international levels."; see Statement by 17 Special Procedures mandate-holders of the Human Rights Council on the Post-2015 development agenda, 21.5.2013, http://www.ohchr.org/EN/NewsEvents/Pages/DisplayNews.aspx?NewsID=13341&LangID=E.

[78] See supra Sect. 3.3.

De Schutter O, Sepúlveda M (2012) Underwriting the Poor. A Global Fund for Social Protection, Briefing note. http://www.ohchr.org/Documents/Issues/Food/20121009_GFSP_en.pdf. Accessed 07 Oct 2012

Engelhardt M (2010) The Millennium Development Goals and Human Rights at 2010—An Account of the Millennium Summit Outcome. GoJIL 2:1129–1146

European Commission (2010) European Instrument for Democracy and Human Rights (EIDHR) Strategy Paper 2011–2013, C(2010)2432, Publications Office, Brussels; http://ec.europa.eu/europeaid/what/human-rights/documents/eidhr_strategy_paper_2011_2013_com_decision_21_april_2011_text_published_on_internet_en.pdf

European Union (2013) Report on Development 2013. Post-2015: Global Action for an Inclusive and Sustainable Future. Publications Office, Brussels. http://www.erd-report.eu/erd/report_2012/documents/FullReportEN.pdf

FCO (2013) Human Rights and Democracy Report 2013. FCO, London. https://www.gov.uk/government/publications/human-rights-and-democracy-report-2013

Global Fund (2014) Global Fund Information Note: Human Rights for HIV, TB, Malaria and HSS Grants. Geneva. http://www.theglobalfund.org/en/about/humanrights/

Global Fund (2011) The Global Fund Strategy 2012–2016—Investing for Impact. Geneva. http://www.theglobalfund.org/en/about/strategy/, Paras 70–75

Global Policy Forum Europe, terre des hommes eds (2013) Globale Nachhaltigkeitsziele für die Post-2015-Entwicklungsagenda; https://www.globalpolicy.org/images/pdfs/GPFEurope/Report_Globale_Nachhaltigkeitsziele_Online.pdf

Gready P, Ensor J eds (2005) Reinventing Development? Translating Rights-based Approaches from Theory into Practice. Zed Books, London

Hamm B (2001) A Human Rights Approach to Development. HRQ 23:1005–1031

Hickey S, Mitlin D (eds) (2009) Rights-Based Approaches to Development: Exploring the Potential and Pitfalls. Kumarian Press, Sterling, VA

Higgins K (2013) Reflecting on the MDGs and making sense of the post-2015 development agenda. The North-South Institute, Ottawa. http://www.nsi-ins.ca/wp-content/uploads/2013/05/2013-Post-2015.pdf

HLP (2013) A New Global Partnership: Eradicate Poverty and Transform Economies through Sustainable Development. United Nations Publications, New York. http://www.post2015hlp.org/wp-content/uploads/2013/05/UN-Report.pdf

HLPE (2012) Social protection for food security. A report by the High Level Panel of Experts on Food Security and Nutrition of the Committee on World Food Security, Rome. http://www.fao.org/fileadmin/user_upload/hlpe/hlpe_documents/HLPE_Reports/HLPE-Report-4-Social_protection_for_food_security-June_2012.pdf

Holtz U (2010) Die Millenniumsentwicklungsziele – eine gemischte Bilanz. Aus Politik und Zeitge-schichte 10:3–9

ILO (2011) Social protection floors for social justice and a fair globalization. Report for the 101st International Labour Conference 2012, ILC 101/IV/1. International Labour Office, Geneva. http://www.ilo.org/wcmsp5/groups/public/—ed_norm/—relconf/documents/meetingdocument/wcms_160210.pdf

ILO (2014) World Social Protection Report 2014/15. Building economic recovery, inclusive development and social justice. International Labour Office, Geneva; http://www.ilo.org/wcmsp5/groups/public/—dgreports/—dcomm/documents/publication/wcms_245201.pdf

Janus H, Keijzer N (2013) Post 2015: How to Design Goals for (Inter)National Action? German Development Institute/Deutsches Institut für Entwicklungspolitik (DIE)- Briefing Paper 23/2013. http://www.die-gdi.de/uploads/media/BP_23_2013.pdf

Kaltenborn M (2013) The Human Rights-Based Approach to Social Protection. In: Bender K et al (eds) Social Protection in Developing Countries. Reforming Systems. Routledge, Abingdon, pp 53–62

Karimova T (2014) The Nature and Meaning of 'International Assistance and Cooperation' under the International Covenant on Economic, Social and Cultural Rights. In: Riedel et al (eds)

Economic, Social, and Cultural Rights in International Law. Contemporary Issues and Challenges. Oxford University Press, Oxford, pp 163–192

Kaul I (2013) Global Public Goods. A concept for framing the Post-2015 Agenda? German Development Institute/Deutsches Institut für Entwicklungspolitik (DIE)-Discussion Paper 2/2013. http://www.die-gdi.de/uploads/media/DP_2.2013.pdf

Kulke U et al (2007) Changing Tides: A Revival of a Rights-Based Approach to Social Security. In: van Langendonck J (ed) The right to social security. Intersentia, Antwerp, pp 13–36

MacNaughton G (2013) Beyond a Minimum Threshold: The Right to Social Equality. In: Minkler L (ed) The State of Economic and Social Human Rights. A Global Overview. Cambridge University Press, Cambridge, pp 271–305

Langford M et al (eds) (2013) The Millennium Development Goals and Human Rights: Past, Present and Future. Cambridge University Press, Cambridge

Liebert N (2011) No Social Justice without Social Protection: What Can International Development Cooperation Do to Make the Social Protection Floor Initiative Work?, Friedrich-Ebert-Stiftung, Dialogue on Globalization 2011. http://library.fes.de/pdf-files/iez/08519.pdf

Loewe M (2010) Entwicklungspolitik, Armutsbekämpfung und Millennium Development Goals. In: Faust J, Neubert S (eds) Wirksamere Entwicklungspolitik. Befunde, Reformen, Instrumente. Nomos, Baden-Baden, pp 101–135

Loewe M (2012) How to Reconcile the Millennium Development Goals (MDGs) and the Sustainable Development Goals (SDGs)? German Development Institute/Deutsches Institut für Entwicklungspolitik (DIE)- Briefing Paper 18/2012. http://www.die-gdi.de/uploads/media/BP_18.2012.pdf

Loewe M (2014) Millennium Plus or Sustainable Development Goals: How to Combine Human Development Objectives with Targets for Global Public Goods? Global Review Summer 2014. http://en.siis.org.cn/index.php?m=content&c=index&a=show&catid=77&id=144

Manning R (2009) Using indicators to encourage development. Lessons from the millennium development goals. Danish Institute for International Studies, Copenhague. http://subweb.diis.dk/graphics/Publications/Reports2009/DIIS_Report_2009-1_Using_indicators_to_encourage_development.pdf

Marks St P (2014) Prospects for Human Rights in the Post-2015 Development Agenda. In: Kozma J et al (eds) Vienna+20. Advancing the Protection of Human Rights. Achievements, Challenges and Perspectives 20 Years after the World Conference. Neuer Wissenschaftlicher Verlag, Vienna, pp 291–306

Melamed C (2012) After 2015: Contexts, politics and processes for a post-2015 global agreement on development. ODI, London. http://www.odi.org/sites/odi.org.uk/files/odi-assets/publications-opinion-files/7537.pdf

Mestrum F (2014) The Compatibility between ILO Recommendation 202 on Social Protection Floors and the ICESCR. In: UNRISD resource platform "Linking Social Protection and Human Rights". http://www.unrisd.org/UNRISD/website/newsview.nsf/(httpNews)/04D1563A3A5FE9D3C1257CCF0044B9DC?OpenDocument

Nelson PJ (2007) Human Rights, the Millennium Development Goals, and the Future of Development Cooperation. World Dev 35:2041–2055

OECD/DAC (2007) Action-Oriented Policy Paper on Human Rights and Development. OECD, Paris. http://www.oecd.org/dac/governance-development/39350774.pdf

Ratjen S, Satija M (2014) Realizing Economic, Social, and Cultural Rights for All. In: Riedel et al (eds) Economic, Social, and Cultural Rights in International Law. Contemporary Issues and Challenges. Oxford University Press, Oxford, pp 111–133

Sano H-O (2007) Does Human-Rights Based Development make a Difference? In: Salomon ME et al (eds) Casting the Net Wider: Human Rights, Development and New Duty Bearers. Intersentia, Antwerp, pp 63–80

Schmidt-Traub G (2009) The Millennium Development Goals and human rights-based approaches: moving towards a shared approach. Int J Hum Rights 13:72–85

Seppänen S (2005) Possibilities and Challenges of the Human Rights-Based Approach to Development, The Erik Castrèn Institute Research Reports 17/2005

Sepúlveda M, Nyst C (2012) The Human Rights Approach to Social Protection. Ministry for Foreign Affairs of Finland, Erweko Oy. http://www.ohchr.org/Documents/Issues/EPoverty/HumanRightsApproachToSocialProtection.pdf

Siebold Th (2008) Armutsorientierte Entwicklung mithilfe von PRSPs? Eine Zwischenbilanz für Subsahara-Afrika, INEF-Report 95/2008; http://inef.uni-due.de/cms/files/report95.pdf

UNDG (2003) The Human Rights Based Approach to Development Cooperation. Towards a Common Understanding Among UN Agencies. United Nations, New York. http://www.undg.org/archive_docs/6959-The_Human_Rights_Based_Approach_to_Development_Cooperation_Towards_a_Common_Understanding_among_UN.pdf

UNHCHR (2013) Who will be Accountable? Human Rights and the Post-2015 Development Agenda. United Nations, New York. http://www.ohchr.org/Documents/Publications/WhoWillBeAccountable.pdf

UNICEF (2012) Integrated Social Protection Systems: Enhancing equity for children. UNICEF, New York. http://www.unicef.org/socialprotection/framework/files/UNICEF_SPSFramework_whole_doc(1).pdf

United Nations (2014) The Millennium Development Goals Report 2014. United Nations, New York; http://www.un.org/millenniumgoals/2014%20MDG%20report/MDG%202014%20English%20web.pdf

USAID (2013) Strategy for Democracy, Human Rights and Governance (DRG). USAID, Washington, D.C. http://www.usaid.gov/sites/default/files/documents/1866/USAID%20DRG_%20final%20final%206-24%203%20%281%29.pdf

Vetterlein A (2007) Economic Growth, Poverty Reduction, and the Role of Social Policies: The Evolution of the World Banks Social Development Approach. Glob Gov 13:513–533

Walker R (2013) Conclusion: towards the analysis of social policy in a developing world. In: Surender R, Walker R (eds) social policy in a developing world. Edward Elgar Publishing, Cheltenham, pp 258–284

Wilson B (2009) Social determinants of health from a rights-based approach. In: Clapham A et al (eds) Realizing the right to health. Rüffer & Rub, Zürich, pp 60–79

World Bank (2012) Resilience, Equity, and Opportunity. The World Bank Social Protection and Labor Strategy 2012–22. World Bank, Washington, D.C. http://siteresources.worldbank.org/SOCIALPROTECTION/Resources/280558-1274453001167/7089867-1279223745454/7253917-1291314603217/SPL_Strategy_2012-22_FINAL.pdf

World Bank/OECD (2013) Integrating Human Rights into Development, 2nd edn. World Bank, Washington, D.C

Index

M. Kaltenborn, *Social Rights and International Development*,
SpringerBriefs in Law, DOI 10.1007/978-3-662-45352-0

MIX
Papier aus verantwortungsvollen Quellen
Paper from responsible sources
FSC® C105338

If you have any concerns about our products,
you can contact us on
ProductSafety@springernature.com

In case Publisher is established outside the EU,
the EU authorized representative is:
Springer Nature Customer Service Center GmbH
Europaplatz 3, 69115 Heidelberg, Germany

Printed by Libri Plureos GmbH
in Hamburg, Germany